Anguish
and
the
Word

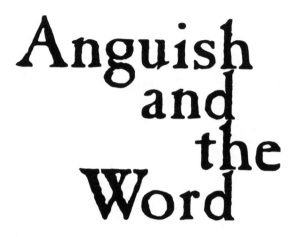

Anguish and the Word

Preaching That Touches Pain

by
David Nelson Duke
and
Paul D. Duke

Smyth
Helwys | &

Anguish and the Word

ISBN 0-9628455-9-0

Anguish and the Word:
Preaching That Touches Pain
Copyright ©1992
Smyth & Helwys Publishing, Inc.

Library of Congress Cataloging-in-Publication Data

Duke, David Nelson
    Anguish and the word: preaching that touches
pain / by David Nelson Duke and Paul D. Duke.
    x + 102 pp.   6 × 9″ (15 × 23cm.)
    Includes bibliographical references.
    ISBN 0-9628455-9-0 : $10.95
    1. Suffering—Religious aspects—Christianity.
2. Preaching. 3. Suffering—Religious aspects—
Christianity—Sermons. 4. Sermons, American.
5. Baptists—Sermons. 6. Presbyterian Church—
Sermons.   I. Duke, Paul D. II. Title.
BT732.7.D85   1992
252′.56—dc20   91-42604
                                        CIP

Contents

Acknowledgements vii

Introduction ix

Part One
Contexts

1 The Pastoral-Liturgical Context of Preaching to Pain:
The Preacher as Shepherd 3

2 The Theological-Ethical Context of Preaching to Pain:
Holiness and the Holy One 21

Part Two
Practice
Illustrative Sermons and Commentary

3 Woman, Your Son
John 19:25-27 49

4 Seeing God in Shadows and Light
Genesis 32:3-31 55

5 The Tree, the Cave, and Beyond
1 Kings 19:1-18 63

6 Called to be Servants, Not Problem-Solvers
Mark 9:30-37; James 3:13-18 69

7 On Not Sulking through the Inevitable
Philippians 4:10-13 77

8 God's People Are True Healers
Luke 10:25-37; Colossians 1:9-12 83

9 Three Faces of Easter
John 20:1-18 91

10 Cultivating Passionate Faith
Mark 1:35-45; 11:15-17 97

Acknowledgments

Though authors thrive on solitude at the creative stage, they are, of course, always in debt to communities of which they are members. The sermons in part two emerged in the context of the hopes and needs of particular congregations: for Paul Duke, Highland Baptist Church in Louisville, Kentucky, and Kirkwood Baptist Church in St. Louis, Missouri; for David Duke, First Presbyterian Church, Liberty, Missouri (during an interim pastorate) and the community of students, staff, and faculty who gathered for a Holy Week service at William Jewell College.

Some of the material in chapter 1 found earlier expression in an assigned article, "Preaching to the Traumatized," in *Faith and Mission* (Fall 1985), a journal of Southeastern Baptist Theological Seminary. There are also echoes from the H. I. Hester Lectures in Preaching at Golden Gate Theological Seminary and at Midwestern Baptist Theological Seminary. The author is grateful to these two institutions for their generous hospitality and encouragement.

—PDD

The first draft of chapter 2 was written during a sabbatical provided by William Jewell College, and the author continues to be grateful to the school for these opportunities for personal and scholarly development. The research for that sabbatical focused on the ways in which the historical Free Church's worship forms, especially its hymnody, attended to pain. In the process it was inevitable that proclamation became part of those reflections. The author is also in debt not only to the research and publications of Professor Samuel E. Balentine, but also his numerous and patient conversations. His work on prayer in the Hebrew Bible, especially his careful and sensitive readings of prayers which grow out of pain, plus his encouragement as a dear friend have been irreplaceable resources for my contributions here.

—DND

Finally, we extend our hearty thanks to Betty Pourcho. Her kindness and skill in preparing the manuscript was a gracious gift to us both.

David Nelson Duke
Paul D. Duke
1991

Introduction

There is no shortage of pain and no shortage of preaching which tries to speak to that pain. The question is, How well does the latter connect with the former?

This book intends to deal with this question practically. By "practical" we do not mean to focus on homiletical and pastoral techniques, though that is part of the discussion. By "practical" we mean careful reflection on and suggestions about the matter of attending to pain in its necessary context of practiced ministry in light of that ministry's theological, ethical, liturgical, and pastoral foundations.

By "practical" we also mean to offer some sermons which illustrate the concerns of our reflections on practiced ministry. We realize the limitations of this inasmuch as sermons are aural events; they are relational—shared between preacher and congregation; and they are contextual—addressing the needs of a particular people in a particular time and place. Still, in hearing and reading about matters related to preaching, the reader and listener may nod in agreement, but wonder, "Yes, but how does that happen? Give me an example." Therefore we offer some carefully selected sermons, which have been preached, with brief introductions of how they illustrate our concerns. Indeed, the fact that they were preached to a particular people at a particular time and place does make the point which is central to our reflections on preaching which touches pain: preaching must be personal and yet not be so imprisoned by a particular context that it diminishes the eternal words of comfort and hope which all of God's people need to hear.

The reflections and sermons are the work of two persons,

brothers in blood, friendship, faith, and ministry. Our working contexts are different, a difference we understand to be an advantage for this project. We are both ministers and theologians, but one functions in the local congregation; the other, in academia. We both ground our faith in worship: one usually as worship leader and preacher; the other, usually from pewside but occasionally from the pulpit. Both regularly interact with people in pain: one as a pastor in a local congregation; the other as teacher and minister in a college setting. Both have known among family and friends some of the wounds of normal human experience and are grateful for many afflictions which have been spared.

The first two chapters reflect our particular contexts and expertise, and the chapter titles indicate this: the first addressing the pastor-liturgical context; the second, the theological-ethical context. And yet the reader will discover that neither chapter is bereft of the other's concerns. In fact, it is our intention that the lines not be drawn very distinctly, for preaching that touches pain must not separate the pastoral, liturgical, theological, and ethical domains. They are a seamless garment for people in pain because they are inseparable in human life and Christian faith.

In the end this is a book not so much about preaching but about the Church, for preaching only has validity and meaning in the context of the full life and mission of the faith community. Therefore it is appropriate that this book be dedicated to the man and woman who have most helped us understand by their words and actions the value of life shaped among God's people. From pulpit and pew, at graveside and bedside, in office or living room—this man and woman understood and consistently practiced the mission of Christ's Church to people in pain. Their character, piety, commitments, and relational skills have sustained and inspired many people, no doubt, more than their humility can imagine. We celebrate a long ministry full-filled. We celebrate a race well run but a journey not yet complete for G. Nelson Duke and Wilma Awbrey Duke.

Part One

Contexts

The Pastoral-Liturgical Context of Preaching to Pain: The Preacher as Shepherd

Imagine yourself in a dream. You are a preacher. In your dream it is Sunday morning and the church service is in progress. It is time for you to speak. You enter the pulpit before a gathering of people who gaze up at you, waiting for your word. Before you begin, you look at them. They are ordinary Sunday morning faces: female and male, old and young, all scrubbed and poised and made up to their best. And, since it is a dream, let us even say these faces are turned up toward you with an actual eagerness for what you are about to say.

Having gathered them with your eyes, you look down to your notes, find your place, whisper a prayer. Then you raise your head to begin—but you freeze in horror at the vision now before you. Now you are in a nightmare. All the people in the pews are grotesquely wounded. Some are cut and bleeding. Some have broken bones and hideous bruises. There are surface abrasions and deep lacerations, bandaged injuries and open gashes bleeding. The people's faces are twisted with pain, and their haunted eyes reach up toward you like clutching hands. Unable to bear it, you drop your gaze.

You swallow hard. You realize you must offer some kind of word. Again you lift your face—and again you stop, astonished. They have become ordinary Sunday morning faces again, scrubbed and poised and lifted with pleasant expectancy. But now you have seen them—what will you say?

The preacher who partakes of a congregation's life, who sits down with them to hear their confession, cheer their victories, taste their disappointments, and enter into intercession for them will know that every sermon is addressed to traumatized people. *Trauma* is the Greek word for wound. No Sunday comes that does not set before the preacher some community of the traumatized. Sometimes the pain grips all the people together, as when the community itself has suffered catastrophe and the people gather in shared shock. On most weeks, however, the wounds are born in separate secrecy and silence throughout the congregation: grief, illness, pain, guilt, depression, joblessness, economic anguish, abandonment, family estrangement, moral failure, impending death. What is more, the preacher knows that whenever the worshiping community gathers, the room is haunted by the pains of those not present in any church—traumatized friends and strangers for whom the congregation is called to become good news. How does the preacher faithfully mediate the gospel to such depth and diversity of pain?

At times the choice may be to preach sermons directed specifically to one or more of these afflictions. A careful sermon on divorce or a series of sermons on death and grief may give long remembered gifts. As a rule, however, the preacher should resort to this method only rarely, if at all. Such preaching in the first place tends to be topical, and preachers are on shaky ground who stand upon topics rather than texts. Furthermore, the preacher whose sermons are usually centered on the traumas of the people will risk preaching a truncated gospel, too reactive, too utilitarian, too small. How easy it is these days in worship to acquiesce to "the triumph of the therapeutic,"[1] to play a kind of psychosociological ping-pong with some Crisis of the Week, offering therapeutic insights rather than "the breadth and length and height and depth" of the gospel.

Preaching that orbits the issues of human pain runs many idolatrous risks. It often distorts scripture by proceeding not from

---

[1]David G. Buttrick has offered a helpful critique of the American pulpit's participation in "the triumph of the therapeutic." See *Homiletic: Moves and Structures* (Philadelphia: Fortress Press, 1987) esp. 31, 273, 422.

Scripture's agenda but from our own. It regularly distorts faith, shifting the center from God to ourselves, abandoning concern for corporate obedience, shrinking the gospel to the petri dish of personal problem solving. What is more, such preaching is inclined to forget those listeners who are not at all traumatized, whose present circumstance is strength, whose need for the gospel lies less in their pain and more in their gifts and opportunities. William Muehl recently complained that, "Human vitalities have been too often treated by the pulpit more as liabilities than as assets."[2] And as Joseph Sittler observed, "whereas we have a gospel for the alienated, the hurt, the depressed, the defeated, we have not a gospel for the well, the effective, the joyous, busy, engaged [folk] of this world."[3] Although preaching in my own Baptist denominational tradition has hardly presented as clear a gospel for the wounded as Sittler describes, his point stands. We cannot sing hope to the afflicted and neglect to sing God's claim on the unafflicted. We must see more than the wounds. Our preaching has its beginning and its center elsewhere.

The most effective proclamation to the whole congregation— the strong and the weak, the wounded and the unscathed—will be a discipline of regular preaching from the Scriptures, expounding upon all the themes of the gospel, making certain as we do so to maintain a vigilant pastoral watch upon the wounds of those addressed by the Word. Use of the lectionary provides a framework for such a systematic program; other plans may also serve. Whatever the particular plan, regular preaching from a full range of biblical texts has power to heal because instead of being an immediate need scrambling for a relevant word, it will be a prior Word faithfully touching real needs—and perhaps redefining what the real needs really are. Fred Craddock has spoken of

---

[2]William Muehl, *Why Preach? Why Listen?* (Philadelphia: Fortress Press, 1986) 41.

[3]Joseph Sittler, *The Anguish of Preaching* (Philadelphia: Fortress Press, 1966) 38; cited by Thomas G. Long, *The Witness of Preaching* (Louisville: Westminster/John Knox, 1989) 33-34. William H. Willimon makes the same point in *The Gospel for the Person Who has Everything* (Valley Forge: Judson Press, 1978) passim.

this redeeming "distance" in proclamation.

> For the message, distance preserves its objectivity as history, its
> continuity as tradition, and its integrity as a word that has ex-
> istence prior to and apart from me as a listener. . . . I am much
> more inclined toward a message that has its own intrinsic life
> and force and that was prepared with no *apparent* awareness of
> me than toward a message that obviously did not come into being
> until I as a listener appeared and then was hastily improvised
> with a desire for relevance. . . .[4]

In a similar vein, H. Stephen Shoemaker has argued that neither "people-directed" preaching nor "preacher-directed" preaching will be as transforming as preaching that recreates the biblical
world and permits that world to cast a healing light upon our
own.[5] Although the preacher may occasionally seize an opportunity to speak in directed response to particular crises, the greatest opportunity for transforming wounded lives will lie in the
week by week shaping of a congregation's consciousness by systematic pastoral proclamation of Scripture, which anticipates all
our diseases.

The question at hand is how to do it. In the course of preaching systematically from biblical texts, what homiletical disciplines will make our sermons more redemptive of human hurt?
The dimension of preaching that concerns us here is frequently
called the "pastoral" dimension. Unfortunately, this designation,
pastoral, is often applied only to the gentler, "softer" forms of response to congregational pain. Thomas G. Long has recently offered a searching critique of what generally passes for "pastoral"
preaching.[6] He observes that such preaching has the positive values of taking the listener seriously, making use of communication strategies, acknowledging the relationship of preacher to
people, and understanding the gospel as being "good news *for us.*"
He also locates the limits of such preaching in overindividualiz-

---

[4]*Overhearing the Gospel* (Nashville: Abingdon, 1978) 121-22.

[5]H. Stephen Shoemaker, *Retelling the Biblical Story: The Theology
and Practice of Narrative Preaching* (Nashville: Broadman, 1985).

[6]Long, *The Witness of Preaching,* 30-36.

ing the gospel, overworking "the notion of relevance," "reducing theology to anthropology," and typically misusing the Bible. His critique of "pastoral" preaching so understood, and so often practiced, is painfully accurate. Still the word *pastoral* has a broader, stronger significance than its misuse would imply. It carries all the rich and wise associations bound up in the metaphor of the Shepherd. It remains a worthy word, and properly understood, a worthy way of faithfully preaching the whole gospel.

Perhaps a good way to explore the principles and methods of pastoral preaching to the traumatized would be to reflect upon this metaphor. Let us think of pastoral preaching in terms of four functions of a shepherd: the functions of gathering, guarding, feeding, and leading.

Gathering

To be wounded is to feel alone. The pain of all anxiety, the pain of all grief down at its root is the pain of isolation. No matter that countless others are members of "the fellowship of suffering," no matter that compassionate friends may already be moving to console, no matter that God's heart is always the first to break, the *experience* of devastation is most often the experience of being wrapped in a numbing cocoon of loneliness. And most of us are in the habit of keeping our wounds to ourselves.

So there the people sit in the pews with their unutterable secrets and their private pain; and how do they experience the corporate worship of God? Most often "from the outside looking in." They are wistful observers, numb spectators. Others know the blessing, others have their places at the table, move easily in the dance. The wounded have no invitation to the party. At its painful outset, at least, worship for them is watching from the wall.

What do they need? They need to hear their names being called. They need to experience the gospel's great inclusiveness of the wounded. This gift is given when those who lead in worship will simply, plainly give utterance to the hidden cries of the human heart. When the preacher names the realities of human pain, the wounded hear their names being called. They recognize themselves in Church—expected and included.

How is this done? By preaching biblically. The Word of God names all secrets, tells all sorrows. Everyone is there: the glad and the guilty, the angry and the sorrowing, the sick and the dying, conquerors, victims, sinners, and fools. The Bible is a procession of so many men and women who went before us bearing all our afflictions. It is the testament of how the living God heard them and moved to address them. The wounded can recognize themselves in Church because they can recognize themselves —everywhere—in the Church's Book. The faithful preaching of biblical texts calls everyone's name.

We need not do this with a heavy hand: "We too are like this leper . . . " or "Now look here, this means you!" All we need do is preach the texts without shrinking from the pain they address. In preaching from a psalm of lament or a prophetic oracle full of pathos or a Bible story that turns on a crisis (name one that doesn't!), to give thoughtful, empathetic description of the human hurt at hand will be enough to gather the wounded in attendance. We simply stand the leper before them and let them see. Making use of simple, vivid, and contemporary expression, we say how it feels inside the disease. And invisibly throughout the congregation hands will go up: "That's my heart you're naming."

This is not possible, of course, if the preacher is unfamiliar with the contours of human suffering. More is needed than the knowledge of newspapers and textbooks. What is needed is the patient will to identify oneself with wounded people. Such identification is obviously an outgrowth of attentive pastoral contact; there is no substitute for time spent listening to the traumatized. But as important as pastoral contact is pastoral imagination; there is no substitute for time spent in the intercessory, priestly act of asking: What must it feel like to be . . . ?[7] But as important as pastoral imagination is the pastor's careful knowledge of his or her own heart; there is no substitute for having traced the contours of our own fears and griefs, and permitting that awful knowledge to instruct us in how to speak to our fellow lepers. These three disciplines—pastoral contact, pastoral imagination,

---

[7]See Fred B. Craddock, *Preaching* (Nashville: Abingdon, 1985) 97-98.

and pastoral self-knowledge —enable the pastoral preacher to give faithful voice to the human pain articulated in the scriptures. Such articulation serves to call the names of the wounded and gathers them into the family of the Word.

In the film *Rain Man,* the actor Dustin Hoffman played the part of an autistic man named Raymond. Among the millions who saw this film was one twelve-year-old autistic boy in California. This boy lived not only in the withdrawal of autism, but apparently suffered as well from a sense of profound embarrassment and shame at his condition. When he and his mother had seen the film, he broke his silence to say: "I'm free now. Thank you, Rain Man." The hardest part of much pain is bearing the loneliness of it. When the wounded recognize themselves in the testaments of people like them, there is a first glimmer of good news. They are gathered in from isolation into the beginnings of community.

Of course, it is not just a matter of recognizing oneself, but of recognizing a multitude of other selves whose pain the Scriptures are also naming. When in worship we gather the wounded, we reach far beyond the immediate and visible circle. Those within that circle should hear not only the name of their own hurt in the preached Word. They should sense that many other names are being called, both within the congregation and far beyond. Real pastoral preaching not only gathers individual sufferers into the community of faith; it also gathers the community of faith into solidarity with the suffering of many others.

Let it be remembered that the preacher is concerned with three realms of pain. There is first the pain of the congregation. This is the pain we know most intimately; we are married to it, and can trace its lines in the faces of those to whom we preach. But the congregation is not our only constituency. Every preacher has a second constituency of people outside the Church who are God's concern and therefore the Church's concern: the poor, the powerless, the neglected, the abused, those who need clearly to hear and to see the gospel and have not.[8] The preacher may not know many of them personally; they may never come to church,

---

[8]This way of describing the preacher's "other constituency" I first heard in a lecture by Ernest Campbell.

and millions of them live in far places. But their pain is the preacher's concern, and it finds a voice in the preaching. The preacher is their advocate before the Church and calls the Church to a faithful response. And there is yet a third realm of pain that concerns the preacher: it is the pain of God. God's pain, of course, participates in the pain of these others. But it is also a larger anguish, for God knows not only the pain that is, but the pain that is yet to be because of the terrible seeds we are planting. This pain must also find a voice in preaching.

The novelist José María Arguedas, in his novel *Deep River,* describes a Peruvian cathedral and a figure of Christ in it called the Lord of the Earthquakes. This Christ has an Amerindian face full of unspeakable sorrow. Arguedas speaks through the character Ernesto:

> The face of the crucified Christ was dark and gaunt . . . Blackened, suffering, the Christ maintained a silence that did not set one at ease. He made one suffer; in such a vast cathedral, in the midst of the candle flames and the daylight that filtered down dimly, the countenance of the Christ caused suffering, extending it to the walls, to the arches and columns, from which I expected to see tears flow.[9]

This gaze of Christ looks upon all our worship. And all our worship, with all our preaching, should burn with this gaze, which not only receives our suffering, but causes us to suffer.

As we have already observed, preaching that articulates the pain of the congregation is often labeled, "pastoral preaching." Preaching that articulates the pain of others and the pain of God is called "prophetic preaching." These distinctions are unfortunate. Biblical preaching to pain gathers all anguish together and is at once both pastoral and prophetic. When preaching embraces the prophetic and forgets to be pastoral, the sermons are shrill and the church is a milling of strangers. When preaching embraces

---

[9]José María Arguedas, *Deep River,* English trans. (Austin: University of Texas Press, 1978), cited by Gustavo Gutiérrez, in *On Job: God-Talk and the Suffering of the Innocent,* trans. Matthew J. O'Connell (Maryknoll NY: Orbis Books, 1987) xvi.

the pastoral and forgets to be prophetic, the sermons are syrup and the church is a klatch of narcissists. The biblical word to the wounded is a larger, more transforming inclusion. Describing our pain, it points to the pain of others. Calling us to their pain, it brings us to the healing of our own. And over all that hurts or is hurtful, it sets the great gathering anguish of God. Authentic pastoral preaching to pain gathers wounded listeners into a church, gathers the church to a wounded world, and gathers all to the wounded Lord.

One method by which the preacher performs the gathering function of pastoral preaching is the use of language that is inclusive. Commitment to inclusive language is more than a matter of being right, it is a matter of being a shepherd. The Word we serve is a gathering Word, with arms as big as the world. Jesus spoke of God's love as like a shepherd who will leave ninety-nine sheep to gather one separated lamb to the flock. Language in the service of that love will do the same, speaking the Word with a vigilant inclusion of women, children, disabled persons, single persons, and all other persons whom a careless use of our language might exclude. Pastoral preaching refuses exclusion, makes inclusion its passion and its joy.

Guarding

Palestinian shepherds carried not only the shepherd's crook or staff, by which a lamb might be gathered in, but also the shepherd's rod or club, by which the sheep were protected from many harms. In the shepherd's bag is a flute for soothing and a sling for killing. Similarly, pastoral preaching to the wounded is not only inclusive, it is protective; it not only gathers, it guards. By "guarding" I do not mean the function of all preaching that appropriately warns people from harm and seeks to lead them not into temptation but deliver them from evil. The protective function to which I refer here is more specific and more modest: it is the preacher's commitment that, at very least, the preaching itself will not inflict more harm upon the wounded.

It is well to ask of any sermon before preaching it, not only "What good will this do?" but "What harm could this do to people already in pain?" Preaching, especially if it is any good, is dangerous. In the prayers, the Scripture, the music, the silences of worship, many people have lowered their shields and removed layers of the defensive cover they normally wear in the world. Here it may be folded back for awhile, and the child's flesh of our inner self be allowed to breathe. The exposed surface of the soul is often tender. Even old wounds, here naked before God, may be raw. Careless words at such an hour can be brutal. When preachers go blundering into the private places of the human heart with no thought of how the words can wound, some souls will do more than wince; they will quietly close again. Not all sermons will do much "gathering" of the traumatized, simply because not all Scripture pertains to woundedness. But on those days when we do not call them out for healing, let us at least be certain that we do not run them over with insensitivity.

Homiletical hit-and-run usually happens when the preacher oversimplifies the sermon, painting the picture so brightly in the case of God's promise, or so starkly in the case of God's judgment, that the real-live wounded are left with no hope. For example, there are several wonderful biblical narratives about "barren" women giving birth, childless couples suddenly blessed with a child. These are texts calling for sermons that celebrate God's promise and our joy. But the preacher is cruel who does this without careful prior attention to those in the congregation who have chosen childlessness, or who would have given anything to have children but could not, or who had children and saw them die. In the same way there will be sermons lifting up the ideals of marriage, but which must not run roughshod over the widowed, or those whose marriages have failed, or who wanted marriage and were denied, or those who chose singleness. For such sermons to be pastorally sensitive does not call for long excurses exploring every exception and explaining God's "Plan B." The sermon may "die the death of a thousand qualifications." A few careful sentences will usually do— sentences extending grace and hope.

When preaching, for example, from a text that tells of a miraculous healing, the preacher will somewhere include a word with reference to so many of our prayers for healing that have not been answered in this way, with a pastoral assurance of how the grace of God here may also apply. This is a matter simply of being responsible, both pastorally and theologically. When pastors know of particular persons in the congregation whose grief is too raw to hear such texts easily, they are wise to call these persons earlier in the week and to explain what will be preached. Such a call can extend a personal context of care to what might otherwise seem an alienating message. It opens a gentler door through which the grieving can *hear* the proclamation without being ambushed by it, and of course it extends to them the freedom of an informed decision about whether or not to attend.

More broadly important, however, than the insertion of a few inclusive sentences or the making of protective calls, is the issue of a preacher's constant language and tone. In so many subtle and pervasive ways, we communicate care or we do not. We are not indifferent messengers of some body of content, we *bear* God's Word in ourselves. We seek not only to speak what God speaks, but to speak in the way that God speaks.[10] So the word of judgment has anguish in it, the word of sorrow has hope in it, and even the word of bright joy is as George Arthur Buttrick would say, "not far from tears." All that is said should be said as if in the presence of the dying, for so it always is. The fact that they are always before us and that the Mystery we proclaim is always capable of being misapprehended demands the most responsible choosing of the words we speak. Jesus' warning about our accountability for every careless word (Matt 12:36) takes on a new dimension in view of the wounded. Diligent, protective preparation becomes a moral necessity.

Perhaps a word should be added concerning what pastoral guarding of the wounded is not. It is not a forfeiture of confrontational preaching. "Pastoral" preaching is not "soft" preaching. Any healing relationship will have an adversarial aspect. In particular, our great Redeemer remains our great Adversary, and cannot be one apart from the other. So we are back to the indivisibility of the pastoral from the prophetic. Pastoral preaching to traumatized people will not think of leaving them without the

---

[10]See Craddock, *Preaching,* 51-52.

redeeming judgment and correction of God's Word. Otherwise, we join the doomed chorus of preachers who "have healed the wound of my people lightly, saying, 'Peace, peace,' when there is no peace" (Jer 6:14; 8:11). Stripping us of our deceits, denying us our false hopes, warning us against self-circling, demanding our responsibility to live in love, and calling us especially to serving the wounded beyond our walls, the prophetic word is indispensable to our own healing and hope. It will be so, at least, if the preacher, like the prophets and like the Christ, offers the word of judgment in solidarity with the congregation, numbering himself or herself among the transgressors as among the wounded. This identification in judgment and in pain will extend to traumatized people the best guarding of all, not thundered warnings from above, but a faithful presence alongside.

Feeding

A third shepherd's function is feeding. The pastor feeds the people in many ways. Most dramatically, they are fed in the mystery of the Eucharist. But the sermon, like the Supper, is also a feeding. There is deep wisdom in the biblical metaphor of Word as Bread; and, as has already been expressed, the surest strength a preacher can offer to people in crisis is a steady diet of Scripture's word. But how is the word best offered as bread to people in pain? How does the shepherd/physician most effectively make provision for the nourishment and strengthening of the wounded?

The preacher does this by putting the Word-Bread within reach and in simple enough form that they can take it in. One does not feed people on the critical list by spreading the dining room table with exotic, gourmet concoctions and announcing, "Dinner is served—please find your place." One prepares plain, digestible nourishment—the kind most likely to "go down" and "stay down"—and brings it within reach.

So in the first place pastoral preaching is relentlessly ordinary, specific, human. It avoids flying off into rarefied abstraction, works hard at being palatable to plain people. It seeks a way of expression that is recognizable to truck drivers, teenagers, and corporate executives, and that actually functions in their minds.

There will be ample analogy and earthy illustration. Because real people, especially people in pain, are fed less through the cognitive intellect than through the imagination, less through the brain than through the heart, the sermon will do more with images than concepts, offer more parables than propositions. And throughout the process of preparation, the preacher will pause paragraph by paragraph to ask: Will this make sense to someone like Fred, like Agnes? Will it work in the minds of people like Maria and like Bill?[11]

This suggests much about the language of pastoral preaching. It will sound less like a dictionary and more like your mother. Literally, it uses the language learned at mother's knee, the mother tongue, the language of nearness—which in the case of English is Anglo-Saxon, not the Greco-Latin speech that is more artificially, paternally acquired.[12]

Furthermore, it will not be wordy speech that the preacher offers to those in pain. The fat must be cut away, and the word offered lean and spare. For most of us it is real labor to prune our speech of fruitless verbiage: empty phrases and cliches, piled-on parallelisms, useless adjectives, adverbs and polysyllables, not to mention whole nonnutritive paragraphs. The plate is so full of peelings and garnish and fat that the patient gives up on finding the food. Love will do the work of cutting away the noise that does not feed.

Consider the following: "Yea, though I walk through the valley of the shadow of death, I will fear no evil, for thou art with me"; "Come to me, all you who labor and are heavy laden, and I will give you rest"; "They shall hunger no more, neither thirst any more; the sun shall not strike them, nor any scorching heat. For the Lamb in the midst of the throne shall feed them, he will lead them to springs of living water, and God will wipe away every tear from their eyes." What texts speak to pain with more power than

---

[11]For an imaginative account of such a process see Thomas H. Troeger, *Creating Fresh Images for Preaching: New Rungs for Jacob's Ladder* (Valley Forge: Judson Press, 1982).

[12]See Walter J. Ong, *The Presence of the Word* (New York: Simon and Schuster, 1967) 250-51.

these three? But note: these combined texts contain a total of eighty-nine English words, and of those eighty-nine there is not one polysyllable; only fourteen have two syllables; all the rest have only one. People in pain need simple speech. Words to the dying must be simple and earnest as breath.

Which points us as well to this truth: words to the wounded will not be prosey; they will sing, at least a little. Why are the most profoundly comforting texts of the Bible invariably poetic? Because troubled people are not hungry for discourse, but for music, for pictures; they are hungry for the sky. Clearly this does not mean fancy or "pretty" speech. As we have seen, simple and plain is the language that feeds. But simple and plain may have some beauty in it, will in fact have much more beauty than the complicated, artificial intonings too often heard from the pulpit. Without attempting to fashion sermons into works of "art"—which is always fatal to preaching—the pastor is wise who labors to purge the preaching of undisciplined ugliness and who, here and there, lets simple language sing. This may mean, as George Buttrick used to say, putting "ordinary words in extraordinary combination." It will mean some attentiveness to sounds and rhythms that please the ear and surprise the heart. It will mean choosing the words that not only signify, but function with some strength. It will mean language full of metaphor, picture, and story, and language most of all that points beyond itself, that hints of far more than it can say.

Why? Because what wounded people hunger for above all is hope, and this is the language that breathes with hope. Poetic speech takes what is common and lifts it to the uncommon—it does with ordinary words what the gospel does with ordinary pain. Prosey speech says what it has to say and closes the door, but poetic speech opens to some sky. Because the gift of God to the dying is better than words can tell, we tell it with the best words we have.

A word should be said about substance as well as form. We do well to remember what kind of content strengthens traumatized people and what kind does not. Explanations, aphorisms, cheerful advice, and formulas for happiness generally do not. Comfort and courage will more likely come when the preacher clearly confesses present pain, invokes the memory of God's past faithfulness, and proclaims the hope of God's present and future mercy. Confession, memory, and hope are bread for the wounded. Had more of us prayed the psalms of lament, which so often repeat this staple movement of the sufferer's heart, we would not have forgotten what feeds. Confession opens the mouth of the present. Memory nurses at the breast of the past. Hope gets up to take hold of a future. These three are strength for the famished.

So also is silence before the Mystery. As important as what the preacher may say to people in pain is what the preacher leaves unsaid. This is more than a matter of not saying false things, it is a matter of not saying more true things than are needful. Comfort does not say everything it knows; it keeps a certain silence. There is a way of preaching to troubled people that lays a gentle hand on the shoulder and shows them a Hope, without telling it all. The chatty comforters of Job fed him not at all. Unanswerable mysteries from the whirlwind fed him indeed. With this, we are back to the issue of appropriate poetic speech in pastoral preaching: language that points and falls silent. It is finally the Spirit of God that bends to feed the wounded, and our language must know when to whisper and step back for that quieter grace to be given.[13]

Leading

If we were people without a hope, the Church might be a kind of terminal home for the wounded, and the pastoral calling a constant administering of small comforts to the bedfast. But we have a hope, and all the people in our charge have somewhere to go. The shepherd's final function is to lead. Pastoral preaching will gather, guard, and feed—in order to lead persons and communities to new places of faithfulness. What does this suggest concerning how we address traumatized people?

---

[13]As many readers will know, the point being stressed in this paragraph reflects the influence of Fred B. Craddock, whose transforming insights into the preacher's silence and the listeners' freedom are found throughout his work on homiletics.

It suggests that pastoral preaching always sets before the people a vision: a vision of their wholeness in the grace of God and a vision of their own vocation to be healers in the world. In any healing relationship, part of the healer's function is to enable the other to see an alternative reality to the present patterns, to assist in mapping out a new course, and to empower them to be on their way. In Christian proclamation the vision will offer both the eschatological promise of final redemption and the present challenge to get on with the race before us. It will take them to the mountain and point to the far-off promise; it will return them to the earthy path at their feet and help them take steps. Both elements of the vision are crucial and constitute together the transformational dreaming of the people of God. The pastoral preacher will encourage the wounded to dream the dreams of God, will invite them to turn those dreams toward prayer, and will urge them to pursue those dreams with the actual engagements of obedience.

Here again, the "pastoral" and the "prophetic" are inseparable. How can the preacher lead people into their own healing without pointing them to their purpose in the world? They never get well if all they ponder is their own wound. The recovery of God's people has everything to do with lifting their gaze to the pain of others. It has to do, in other words, with repentance.

> Then shall your light break forth like the dawn,
>   and your healing shall spring up speedily. . . .
> If you take away from the midst of you the yoke
>   the pointing of the finger and speaking wickedness,
> if you pour out yourself for the hungry
>   and satisfy the desire of the afflicted,
> then shall your light rise in the darkness
>   and your gloom be as the noonday.   (Isaiah 58:8a, 9b-10)

Led to act upon God's love for all, the congregation learns at last how transforming is God's love for them.

To lead will be to *lead*, not to coerce. There can be no forced marches for the wounded. Pastoral preaching will know how to be direct, but will know also the grace of indirection. Even in "feeding" the people, the preacher does not rush in to do all the business of explanation and application. As Fred Craddock has repeatedly reminded us, it is not the preacher's place to chew the food before the listener swallows it. So in the labor of leading, what the pastor leaves unsaid will be crucial. Suggestion and deliberate silences will give listeners much-needed opportunities to step toward the meaning and offer their own Yes to the claims of the gospel. All people, and especially people in crisis, need to be offered the grace of their own initiative. Pastoral leading from the pulpit will beckon toward a dream but never bludgeon with it. It will not drag the people into the preacher's dream but will show an open door.

The nature of such leadership calls for several kinds of pastoral balance: the balance between talk and silence, the balance between intimacy and distance, the balance between being an adversary with people and being wholeheartedly identified with them, between the courage to be ahead of them and the courage to be at their side. We do well to remember Ezekiel's first order of business with the exiles: "The Spirit lifted me up and took me away . . . and I came to the exiles . . . who dwelt by the river Chebar. And I sat there astonished among them for seven days" (Ezek 3:14-15). We may not speak or lead until we have sat astonished among them. Neither may we sit astonished without finally telling the terrible and glorious vision. Neither can we speak it and not then fall silent again to give them their freedom.

Once more there are implications about the language of preaching, especially where it seeks to set a transforming vision before the people. As with the most "pastoral" biblical texts, so with the most "prophetic"—they are cast without fail into the language of poetry. How else could they speak? They are invoking a new world. They are singing God's invitation to be new creatures. They cannot be prosey; the structures of the old world are prosey. As Walter Brueggemann has said, kings communicate in memos, prophets in poetry.[14] Their vision stirs them to the only kind of language that evokes vision, the language of song.

---

[14]See Walter Brueggemann, *The Creative Word* (Philadelphia: Fortress, 1982) 51-54; also, *Finally Comes the Poet: Daring Speech for Proclamation* (Minneapolis: Fortress Press, 1989) 4 and passim.

And it is not just because they cannot help it, it is because they are wise. A pastoral prophet's poetry is not just ecstasy, it is strategy. Singing the Word is our most subversive act against the prosey powers of this age. And it is our most effective, winsome way of calling out hope to each other, and not pushing people but drawing them into the joy of God's Realm.

In the early 1960's, when racial conflict was beginning its public eruption in the deep south of the United States, a southern white man went down to where the worst conflict was raging. He watched black people claiming their rights and saw them badly beaten. He returned home and a friend asked him about what he had seen. He said it looked bad, that the culture was against them, the law was against them, the F.B.I. was against them. His friend said, "So they're going to lose?" The man said, "No, I think they will win." His friend said, "But you said the culture and the law and the F.B.I. are against them. How can they win?" The man answered, "They have a song." People who are tired and beaten are not led into transformation by lectures or cheery chit-chat. What stands them on their feet and empowers them to take steps is the word with distant music in it. Pastoral preaching to the wounded will impart this gift.

We do not lead them to better feelings, we do not lead them to come back to church, we certainly do not lead them to ourselves. We lead them to go on to God—to obedience, to hope, and to transforming communion with the Holy. This is finally the function of all preaching. This is what leaves us, in the end, embarrassed, grateful, and profoundly unnecessary. We disappear. Abraham Heschel said, "Preach in order to pray."[15] There is no better wisdom for our preaching. We speak to those in pain to take them to the borders of prayer, where God alone may work in them the grace of transformation. If we are wise, this is where we as well, with our own measure of priestly and personal pain, will permit the Word to abandon us.

—PDD

---

[15]Abraham Heschel, *Quest for God* (New York: Crossroads, 1984) 80.

The Theological-Ethical Context of Preaching to Pain: Holiness and the Holy One

George Herbert once wrote that the preacher should not strive to be "witty, or learned, or eloquent, but Holy."[1] The issue for Herbert was not to moralize on the minister's private life and piety, but to claim that even in that most humanly contrived moment in worship—the sermon—the human words and presence of proclamation should be transparent to the Holy One for whom, because of whom, and in whose presence worship takes place.

Holiness appears to be an unlikely entrée into an exploration labeled "Preaching That Touches Pain," for suffering would seem to call for an emphasis on the *benefits* of such preaching for the sufferers, thereby concentrating on what has been called the subjective dimension of worship. That is, one might assume that preaching to pain means focusing on the sermon's *instrumental* value for the sufferers: helping them to cope, consoling them, or providing catharsis in some way.

It will be evident that this subjective dimension is crucial for our discussion, but we must be careful not to regard preaching to pain as a Christianized version of coping skills. In saying that, we do not intend in any way to demean the coping skills which are a valuable part of pastoral care. Rather, the concern here is to identify how the *context of worship* itself can become a context for addressing pain as well as complementing other ministry to

---

[1]George Herbert, *The Country Parson,* ed. John N. Wall, Jr. (New York: Paulist Press, 1981) 63.

pain in the community of faith.

What is at stake here is not playing off the objective side of worship against the subjective, but to assert once again that worship of God, the "object"[2] of our faith, necessarily enriches our experience, the subjective dimension. Or, as John Calvin described it, only by knowledge of God do we come to have knowledge of ourselves.[3] It follows that there ought to be a correspondence between the ways of God and the ways of those who worship and follow that God.

Holiness and the Holy One

Faith is a journey, a journey during which there ought to be growth and development. Faith needs help along the way, not only in times of suffering, but in smoother and even celebrative times when we may be able to reflect on previous experiences of pain and learn better how to be and act as God's people for afflicted persons. This growth in faith is what Christians have called sanctification or holiness.

Our goal is not to cultivate spiritual escapists, but the very opposite: persons who take their own pain seriously, who experience other people's pain deeply and compassionately, who are moved to do something about that pain, and who draw comfort, strength, and motivation from their God who personally knows and responds to that pain. One need not be a Marxist to acknowledge that much of what passes as religion responds to pain with spiritual narcotics, ultimately denying pain's reality and deflecting people from getting at the roots of their suffering. We must be careful not to become dope peddlers, but instead bearers of the Good News, Good News not only for people to hear but Good News to shape their lives. As Stanley Hauerwas argues, Christian faith gives us "the skills rightly to see and act in the world, not as we

---

[2]By speaking of God as "object," we mean that God is the transcendent focus and source of human faith. We do not mean that God is impersonal or an object for manipulation.

[3]John Calvin, *Institutes of the Christian Religion,* vol. 1, trans. Henry Beveridge (Grand Rapids: William B. Eerdman's, 1979) 37-38.

want it to be, but as it is, namely as God's good but fallen creation."[4]

Therefore the question, How can the human words of preaching become transparent to the Word and thereby speak to people in pain?, also becomes the question, How can preaching as an avenue for encountering the Holy One help to cultivate holy people? These holy people of God will

— face their own pain honestly with God, with themselves, and others;
—comprehend the connection between their own pain and other persons' pain;
—take seriously other people and their pain, resisting the temptation to offer simplistic, spiritually sugarcoated advice;
—recognize the connection between personal pain and pain wrought by social and political structures; and
—value the faith community as the appropriate context for addressing and caring for these people in pain.

In essence such preaching aids persons in growing to be like God—holy, a foundational element in the biblical understanding of the God-human relationship. For instance, the collection of laws in Leviticus known as the "Holiness Code" commands, "You shall be holy; for I the Lord your God am holy" (19:2). Appropriately it is this collection of laws which commands love for one's neighbor (19:18) and the stranger (19:34). Like its predecessors this Holiness Code called for care and in this case love based on Israel's experiences of slavery's painful oppression: "you shall love him (the stranger) as yourself; for you were strangers in the land of Egypt" (19:34). Hebrew morality in general, especially its emphasis on care for victims, was grounded in the nation's own experience of suffering. Hence the Holiness Code's command to "love your neighbor as yourself" was not pragmatism, not a theological version of ethical egoism, but an ethic grounded in a common historical experience of pain. Because they had known oppressive suffering firsthand, the Hebrews were to know what love requires for the suffering. It is helpful to recall that Israel's deliv-

---

[4]Stanley Hauerwas, *The Peaceable Kingdom: A Primer in Christian Ethics* (Notre Dame: University of Notre Dame, 1983) 35.

erance from slavery began with a God who "knew (not knew about) their condition" (Exod 2:23-25). This is the context within which we should hear "You shall be holy; for I the Lord your God am holy." To be holy, to be like God, was to be different. What was distinctive about this Hebrew view was not its concern for religion or morality, nor even its special concern for suffering people,[5] but the source and motivation for that care: their historical encounter with their God rooted in their experience as slaves and aliens who had been heard, cared for, and delivered by the Holy One of Israel.

The New Testament portrays the holy life (the sanctified life, life in the Spirit, the new nature) by traits which clearly describe the sort of person who not only cares about those in pain, but one who also feels their pain alongside them. Hebrews 13:3, for example, clearly identifies this way of being: "Remember those who are in prison as though you were in prison with them." This way of being is, of course, consistent with the model offered by Jesus, the Incarnation of the Holy One, who is said to have been viscerally moved to compassion for the bereaved (e.g., Luke 7:13) and hungry (Mark 6:34) and who wept at the death of a friend (John 11:33-36).

Most of us have known persons who embodied these traits, and appropriately we often refer to them as saints (literally, "holy ones"). They have a certain disposition which is acutely attentive to need. They are humble, oriented to service, and selfless. They are not weak-kneed or easily manipulated, and like their Master, they are strong, courageous persons, grounded in a Power who is more than their natural abilities. Most likely, our experience has been that these saints depended profoundly on disciplined worship of their God, for the Holy One became the source of their holiness.

Preaching can help to cultivate such holiness as over the

---

[5]Contrary to popular accounts of Hebrew morality, its concern for the poor, orphans, and oppressed was not unique in Ancient Near Eastern literature. However, the motivation was different: their historical memory of being slaves. They had known oppression and had encountered their God in their deliverance from bondage.

weeks, months, and years sermons are remembered not for their scholarship, wittiness, or eloquence, but because they helped to lead worshippers into the presence of the Holy One. Thus, our preaching should encourage what Geoffrey Wainwright suggests ought to be the result of worship: "the renewal of the vision of the value-patterns of God's Kingdom,"[6] including those characteristics of holy people who attend to their own pain and others' pain with openness, honesty, and genuine, heartfelt care.

Again, this renewal is not a manipulated result, but the overflow of an encounter with the God who has been known through Israel's covenant and through Jesus Christ. The renewal comes not from achieving the "right" forms and effects in worship, but by drinking from the fountain of grace in whose presence the worshipers have communed. If we wish to state the intention of worship from the subjective side, we could do no better than the hope expressed for worship by G. Henton Davies: "All I ask is that for one fleeting moment I be taken into the presence of God."[7]

Like Jacob wrestling with God by the Jabbok ford, to encounter the Holy One in worship is to be altered in one's whole being, perhaps not only renewed, but from time to time gaining a new understanding of God and thereby of oneself. As Abraham Heschel has noted, our encounter is with the Holy One *of* Israel,[8] not an obscure transcendence, but the Holy One who is actively seeking and engaged in relationships.

In her classic work on Christian worship Evelyn Underhill states that "To worship well is to live well."[9] The intended outcome of encountering the Holy One is holiness. Thus the renewal of our vision in worship is not the quick fix for which too many people yearn. Rather, this renewal of vision ought to invigorate the development of faith, for the journey of faith requires training (discipline) in the living of life under God's leadership.

---

[6]Geoffrey Wainwright, *Doxology: The Praise of God in Worship, Doctrine, and Life* (New York: Oxford University Press, 1980) 8.

[7]G. Henton Davies, a public lecture, William Jewell College, 1981.

[8]Abraham Heschel, *The Prophets* (New York: Harper and Row, 1962) 224.

[9]Evelyn Underhill, *Worship* (New York: Harper and Row, 1936) 79.

Faith as a Passionate Journey of the Whole Person

Perhaps it appears that we have traveled too far afield, for earlier we seemed more concerned with the relationship between pastoral care and worship; and now we are relating ethics and worship. Underhill's terminology may help us to break down the artificial divisions which have been created: "To worship well is to *live* well." Is it not obvious that there is or at least should be some connection between our dealing with pain and our moral attitudes and behavior? To appreciate this connection, we must come to terms with the all-too-common tendency to divide human experience into distinct parts, as if there were some ontological schizophrenia defining human nature. Many people tend to focus on one dimension of the human as the essence of faith.

(1) One popular notion equates faith with doctrinal assent. The emphasis is on believing *in* or believing *that* a particular set of doctrines are true. Faith has to do with correct ideas. Rationality is the cornerstone of faith. The opposite of faith is labeled doubt, which includes not only intellectual questioning, but also intellectual confusion. The mind is obviously the primary dimension in this understanding of faith.

Curiously enough, those who invest faith's energy primarily in the intellectual suspicion of doctrine fall in the same camp, though they seem to be at the opposite end of the theological spectrum. These doctrinal minimalists, believing nothing which does not meet the canons of their system of logic, no less than the Fundamentalist or the rigorous Scholastic, share a common view of faith: faith is primarily what the mind believes—whether it be a rigorously defined creed, an inerrant Bible, or a minimalist affirmation. For all of these faith is primarily an act of the human mind.

(2) For others the essence of faith is feeling. For most in this camp faith is associated with a particular emotional event or level of emotional intensity. Thus faith is associated primarily with the experience of conversion, or a "spiritual gift," or a unique experience of God's presence in prayer or meditation. There are also those who identify faith with a particular sense of awe, wonder, or even aesthetic pleasure. For all of these expressions the op-

posite of faith is the absence or loss of the special feeling's intensity. Those who live with this understanding of faith are subject to a rollercoaster effect as the feelings ebb and flow, as they inevitably will.

(3) Faith can also be understood primarily in terms of activity, physical energy, or deeds. Outward human activity becomes the measure of faith. The activity may be deeds supportive of the institutional church, deeds of charity, or the activity of pursuing a particular social and political agenda. The opposite of faith in this frame of reference is inactivity or inferior performance. Like the two previous notions of faith, this faith's authenticity tends to be measured quantitatively. If the quantity of approved deeds or commitments diminishes, so does "faith."

(4) A fourth view of faith focuses on the will. Faith is primarily an affirmative act of the will: perhaps the blind obedience of believing what an institution or a compelling leader advocates, or even just the act of will known as good intentions. This view of faith is more difficult to define, though illustrations make it clear that it not only exists, but flourishes all around us. A television faith healer tells his listeners that if they will just have enough faith (and probably send him $100 as well), they will be delivered from their physical infirmities. It is the will that counts here, not so much the mind, the feelings, or even deeds (though the $100 may help). What matters is that one employs the will deliberately and consistently, so that by having faith *in faith,* healing will take place. A very different sort of faith emphasizing the will is the blessing given or self-bestowed on the person who is charitable in her attitudes, though her actions of charity may not sufficiently reflect these attitudes. People defend themselves and others by statements like, "Well, you know her heart is in the right place." What is being affirmed is an integrity of the will. Institutional and personal loyalty are perhaps the most frequent expressions of faith based on the will. The mind, the feelings, and action ultimately play very small roles in their view of faith.

What these four views of faith share is their focus on one dimension of human experience. They also tend to quantify faith. They advocate a narrow, one-dimensional expression of faith. Each of these dimensions is important, and therefore each of these expressions of faith is partially true. None of them, however, understands faith in terms of the psychosomatic wholeness in which human beings were created and experience life.

(5) We come now to what many would label the "real" definition of faith, and like students who have been led through all the other possibilities, which have been critiqued and discarded, we all raise our hands knowing that this last choice is the correct answer. Yes, the best understanding of faith is one which emphasizes *trust*, but even this traditional definition is fraught with problems if not appropriated carefully. "Trust" can be sentimentalized so that the relationship between God and humans is immature, even syrupy. Or, it can be rendered dualistically so that relationship with God is otherworldly, encouraging apathy rather than the passionate relationship between humanity and *abba* God modeled by Jesus. In both cases the visceral dimensions of human experience are ignored, if not ultimately denied. Thus real pain and its relationship to faith cannot be taken seriously—one's own pain, the pain of other persons, and the pain of God.

It is clear then that faith as trust must be understood in a dynamic way consistent with those countless biblical images which describe faith as a passionate journey pursuing God's way. This definition flies in the face of most popular views of spiritual maturity. In one quarter spiritual maturity is associated with resignation whereby one reaches a level of faith at which nothing phases the believer, no matter what comes. It is all manageable by the person of faith. This is little more than a spiritualized rolling-with-the-punches mentality, a kind of stoical "joy in the Lord." At first glance some might not regard this attitude as problematic, but closer examination reveals the absence of passion. Without passion suffering cannot be understood, for it is not experienced. Dorothee Soelle suggests that the pursuit of a painless life destroys people's ability to feel anything[10] and thus the ability to take seriously and aid the suffering of others. Stoical, passionless trust in God will leave us distant from the pain of other persons and distant from the heart of God, for faith as stoical joy

---

[10]Dorothee Soelle, *Suffering,* trans. Everett R. Kalin (Philadelphia: Fortress, 1975) 4.

has lost the ability to feel with those people and feel with God.

The other most popular notion of spiritual maturity is one which sentimentalizes life so that the best possible face (the "spiritual" side) is imposed on every situation. Every dark cloud has its spiritual silver lining. Therefore the pain of one's own life and the pain of others cannot be taken too seriously. "The Life of Brian," the Monty Python spoof of traditional portraits of Jesus, was not much of a movie, but it did get one parody right. The character Brian, who has parallel experiences to Jesus, is mistaken for another messianic leader and, like Jesus, crucified. Trying to make the best of the bad situation, he and then other crucified persons begin singing, "Look on the sunny side of life." To many believers this is an offensive portrayal, for it tends to trivialize an event Christians have regarded reverently. And yet the trivialization was baptized long before this silly Monty Python farce; for if the popular notion of sentimentalizing suffering were extended to Jesus's crucifixion, the Monty Python troupe was right on target: singing "look on the sunny side of life" from the cross would be the ideal Christian response to pain.

Let us try to get our moorings by recalling the familiar "Great Commandment": "You shall love the Lord your God with all your heart, and with all your soul, and with all your strength, and with all your mind; and your neighbor as yourself" (Luke 10:27). Here is a vision calling for the whole person to love God, the whole person to worship God, the whole person to live with and before God, and the whole person to love the neighbor. What would happen if we consistently presented such a vision of God's Kingdom in our preaching so as to contradict the persistent compartmentalization of human life and Christian faith? What would it mean to preach to pain with this holistic understanding of human life and faith? Issues of theology, pastoral care, ethics, and spirituality might converge. There might be a renewal of this right vision of God's Kingdom. It might help to cultivate holiness in people's lives, holiness which attended to their own pain and others' pain seriously and passionately in the context of faith.

In addition to this view of faith as a passionate journey of the whole person there are two other emphases in preaching which might help to restore this vision and thereby encourage the development of holy lives which attend sensitively and carefully to pain: (1) the pathos and resurrection power of God and (2) the mutual support of the faith community. These are the two pillars undergirding the passionate journey of faith. We begin with the pathos and resurrection power of God, for the primary concern of our preaching is that it be transparent to the Holy One who passionately cares and brings new life in times of joy and pain.

Pathos and the Resurrection Power of God

The question is, To what sort of God do we point in our preaching? Is it the God who takes human pain seriously, who not only knows about human pain but feels and responds to it as well? This is the God to which Scripture— Hebrew Bible and New Testament—testifies. If the human encounter with this Holy One is the foundation of holy lives, then it may not be too crass to suggest that as goes the God, so goes that God's worshipers. A passionless, impersonal God of fate, who cannot identify, feel, and respond to pain, will most likely cultivate passionless, impersonal, inactive followers who have difficulty identifying with, feeling, and responding to the pain of persons with whom they have relationships, much less persons in situations foreign to their experience.

Elie Wiesel recounts the Hasidic tale of a child crying because his playmates have abandoned him during a game of hide-and-seek. The child had hidden himself, but his playmates stopped looking for him. The child felt forsaken and abused. So it is with God, said the master, for God, too, is hiding and grieving because human beings have stopped searching for the divine presence.[11] Wiesel's story works at several levels, but what may be most useful is the way it shakes up traditional notions of the God-human relationship. It suggests that the relationship is an ongoing search or no relationship at all—abandonment of God. It suggests that God needs the relationship with human beings, that God has an investment in that relationship so that abandonment by humans

---

[11]Elie Wiesel, *Four Hasidic Masters and Their Struggle against Melancholy* (Notre Dame: University of Notre Dame, 1978) 52-53.

brings an affective response from God. God is therefore not best understood as the omniscient, omnipotent Mind, but as the personal being with passionate, visceral feelings interacting with human experiences and history.

Abraham Heschel clarifies this approach to God by insisting that attributing pathos to God is not reducing God to crude anthropomorphisms, as the Western preference for mind over body would have us believe. Heschel reminds us of the biblical understanding of God which is foreign to these dualistic assumptions.

> The idea of the divine pathos combining absolute selflessness with supreme concern for the poor and the exploited can hardly be regarded as the attribution of human characteristics. Where is the man who is endowed with such characteristics? Nowhere in the Bible is man characterized as merciful, gracious, slow to anger, abundant in love and truth, keeping love to the thousandth generation.[12]

Thus our preaching needs to employ the "language of presence" (and absence) about God, not the "language of essence."[13]

This biblical understanding of God suggests that the dynamic nature of faith is not limited to a dynamism only on the human side of the relationship, but on God's side as well. If God is not an Unmoved Mover bereft of emotion and change or a glorified Santa Claus who "*sees* you when you're sleeping, . . . *knows* when you're awake, . . . *knows* if you've been bad or good . . . ," then God is affected by and responds to people's experiences in all their dimensions. As Heschel states, a God who is above human responses and therefore beyond anger is an indifferent God, and that indifferent deity is a far cry from the Holy One *of* Israel.

> Events and human actions arouse in Him joy or sorrow, pleasure or wrath. He is not conceived as judging the world in detachment. He reacts in an intimate and subjective manner, and thus determines the value of events. Quite obviously in the biblical view, man's deed may move Him, affect Him, grieve Him, or, on the other hand, gladden and please him. . . . God can be

---

[12]Heschel, *The Prophets,* 271.
[13]Ibid., 275.

intimately affected. . . . He possesses not merely intelligence and will, but also pathos. . . .[14]

The same God manifested in Jesus Christ is no distant God. If we take seriously Jesus's physical pain (crucifixion), emotional pain (abandonment by friends), and spiritual pain (Godforsakenness), then, if indeed Jesus was both human and God as we confess, we can preach no passionless God.

Like the Hasidic tale, this God does grieve that humanity is no longer searching; and many humans grieve as well, for in the hidden depths of their being racked by pain, they are rarely sought out and taken seriously by persons identified with religious communities. In their pain they are frequently offered simplistic aphorisms, like "let go and let God," or quoted paraphrased Scripture verses (usually out of context), "God sends us no more than we can bear." Karl Marx, Sigmund Freud, and other detractors of Christianity were at least partially right: much of what parades under the name of religion is escapism, encouraging people to ignore their lives and the real basis of their pain.

One corrective to this escapism might be preaching which attempts to give fuller expression to the image which Jesus emphasized in describing God and his followers' relationship to God: God as *abba*. It has been beneficial that the visual and cultural dimensions of this image have come under feminist scrutiny, for, in fact, the linkage of *abba* with the traditional father figure very well may not be the freight which the image was intended to carry. The direction of the image seems to be more relational and affective (like either parent) than visual.

Abba connotes a parent who desires intimacy, who has known the other person in the relationship through the struggles of living and growing, who has sustained and cared for the other even when that one ignored the parent. The *abba*-child relationship is one built on a history of personal interactions at more than the cognitive level; such relationships are felt. They are more easily felt than described, like love, for that, too, is a relational term. Pathos is prominent in the *abba*-child relationship. Such rela-

---

[14]Ibid., 224.

tionships expect *shared* joy, sorrow, rejection and anger, forgiveness, reconciliation, and renewed commitment. Whatever the limits of understanding Jesus's parable of the Prodigal Son as an allegory, the parable does communicate the pathos of the *abba*-child relationship in the Kingdom of God.

Preaching which emphasizes the pathos of God cultivates an expectation of God the caregiver, not God the decision-maker. Thus the portrayal of God should be less one of a Being deciding when and what to happen to whom, and more one of a personality with steady, visceral parental care for human beings in all their circumstances. Like a parent who is attentive to the changing needs of her children, God is better understood through the traditional biblical images of mother bird, attentive father, loyal spouse, or nursing mother than an omnipotent decision-maker or even a problem-solver. As the New Testament portrays this in its use of the term *abba*, the direction of the worshipper's prayer is more one of petition for presence and care than an appeal for solutions to problems by the providential decision-maker (e.g., Matt 6:9-13; Rom 8:12-17; Gal 4:6-7).

This emphasis on the passionate care of God ought to have an impact on those who follow that God and seek to be like that God. The model of holiness thus becomes passionate care rather than the human imitation of the omnipotent decision-maker and problem-solver.

This shift in models allows prayer to become more of a relationship between a child of God and *abba*, with an honest expression of feelings offered up to the One who parentally cares. Thus it will be understood that *abba*-God is not offended or surprised to hear complaint, anger, and questions in prayer from *abba*'s children. For too long, the pious prayers of the lament psalms have been regarded as sub-Christian, for they do not put on the face of so-called Christian joy (read resignation). Contrast Psalm 13 with the popular hymns which deny fears and doubts, and one comprehends the stark difference between prayer to *abba*-God and the popular, indifferent God worshipped by too many congregations. Lest Psalm 13 be viewed as a product of "the old dispensation," recall Jesus's prayers in Gethsemane and on the cross.

The passionate God is still the Holy One, more than a God who simply hurts with the suffering, as some contemporary versions of a Theology of the Cross seem to advocate. Preaching must do more than embrace that popular modern theological trend which seems to limit God's care to divine empathy. To be sure, the renewal of understanding God's hiddenness and suffering has been invaluable, for we have come to appreciate that God's being includes vulnerability, the experience of pain, and identification with the suffering. Yet the limitation of this emphasis to God's suffering presence not only misrepresents the Christian tradition but provides limited hope for sufferers. It is clear that Heschel's understanding of the pathos of God is not so limited, for he speaks of God "reacting" to human experience. The pathos of God is not just the shared experiences of pain but also the mysterious and unpredictable possibility for transformation as symbolized by the resurrection of Christ.

Those who minister to people in pain are rightly wary of the resurrection theme, given its easy abuse. If resurrection is the Happy Ending for Jesus and our suffering, then suffering is a problem resolved by human endurance: just holding on long enough to realize the inevitable triumphal conclusion. This silver lining approach lends itself to advocating eschatological compensation: that with all life's trials, there still is the promise of eternal bliss for the sufferer. Again, we are in the realm of escapism.

The promise of resurrection may also encourage otherwise sensitive people to ignore the power of what Simone Weil labels "affliction," a category she distinguishes from suffering.

> It is not surprising that the innocent are killed, tortured, driven from their country, made destitute, or reduced to slavery, imprisoned in camps or cells, since there are criminals to perform such actions. It is not surprising either that disease is the cause of long sufferings, which paralyze life and make it into an image of death, since nature is at the mercy of the blind play of mechanical necessities. But it is surprising that God should have given affliction the power to seize the very souls of the innocent and to take possession of them as their sovereign lord. At the very best, he who is branded by affliction will keep only half his soul. . . .

Affliction makes God appear to be absent for a time, more absent than a dead man, more absent than light in the utter darkness of a cell. A kind of horror submerges the whole soul. During this absence there is nothing to love. What is terrible is that if, in this darkness where there is nothing to love, the soul ceases to love, God's absence becomes final. . . .

Affliction hardens and discourages us because, like a red hot iron, it stamps the soul to its very depths with the scorn, the disgust, and even the self-hatred and sense of guilt and defilement that crime logically should produce but actually does not.[15]

In addition to a sense of God's absence and this wrenching of the soul, affliction has other devastating effects, according to Weil. It makes one feel like an outcast; it encourages self-hatred; it makes one feel "accursed"; it brings on paralysis to the soul, the "poison of inertia." The result is that affliction

deprives its victims of their personality and makes them into things. It is indifferent; and it is the coldness of this indifference—a metallic coldness—that freezes all those it touches right to the depths of their souls. They will never find warmth again. They will never believe any more that they are anyone.[16]

Those who have lived with eyes and hearts open understand Weil's distinction between suffering and affliction. There is a physical dimension to the experience. The tragic death of a loved one can bring on an ache in the cavity of the body which feels as if it will explode, as if the body were about to be wrenched in two. A shattered relationship may bring on the same experience, as if a hole were being burnt in the soul. The old expression, "I felt as if my heart were breaking," is an apt description of pain becoming affliction.

What Weil describes is that which can gnaw away at faith and bring on despair and the loss of faith. The metallic coldness of the indifference bred by affliction is the polar opposite of faith, not the questions or the anger of doubt. In fact, if doubt is evidence of pas-

---

[15]Simone Weil, *Waiting for God,* trans. Emma Crawford (New York: G. P. Putnam's Sons, 1951) 119-21.

[16]Ibid., 122, 125.

sion, there is hope; for where there is passion, there is the opportunity for faith. Passion is evidence that something matters.
Where there is apathy or the crushing despair rendered by affliction, there the ground for faith has hardened.

Perhaps one way to grasp the significance of resurrection for
affliction is to consider one of the most creative juxtapositions of
the crucifixion and resurrection images in worship: Matthias
Grunewald's Isenheim altarpiece. Many have found this 16th
century German artist's rendering of the crucifixion useful for il-
lustrating God's suffering. This portrayal of *kenosis* was well described by a 19th century French essayist, Joris-Karl Huysmans.

> [Christ's body is] dotted with spots of blood, and bristling like a
> chestnut-burr with splinters that the rods have left in the
> wounds; at the ends of the unnaturally long arms the hands twist
> convulsively and claw the air; the knees are turned in so that
> the bulbous kneecaps almost touch; while the feet, nailed on top
> of the other, are just a jumbled heap of muscles underneath rot-
> ting, discoloured flesh and blue toenails; as for the head, it lolls
> on the bulging, sack-like chest patterned with stripes by the cage
> of the ribs. . . . the jaw . . . hangs loosely, with open and slaver-
> ing lips. . . . The Man-God of Colmar [location of the altarpiece]
> is nothing but a common thief who has met his end on the gal-
> lows.[17]

It is not only Grunewald's extraordinary visual portrayal of
Christ as a human sufferer which has captivated the imagination
of moderns but the context of the painting as well. The crucifixion was the central part of an altarpiece in a monastery chapel
which cared for people with a horrid skin disease. Thus the whelps
of the crucified Christ's body closely resembled the affliction of
patients who worshiped there. The existential meaning of Christ's
suffering thereby can be understood to be quite powerful.

What is ignored in theological discussions of Grunewald's
work is his accompanying portrayal of the resurrection, which is
part of the same altarpiece. The panels of the crucifixion open out

---

[17]J. K. Huysman, "The Grunewalds in the Colmar Museum," in
Grunewald: The Paintings (New York: Phaldon Publishers, Inc., 1958)
10-11.

to another set of paintings: the Annunciation on the left; a centerpiece which portrays the adoration of the angels for Mary and the child Christ as mother and child sit in the shimmering light of the ethereal glow of God the Father; and a magnificent rendering of the resurrected Christ on the right.

It is the last of these which requires our attention as a rich contrast to the crucifixion panel. Again, Huysman's description is useful.

> This is a strong and handsome Christ, fair-haired and brown-eyed. . . . All round this soaring body are rays emanating from it which have begun to blur its outline; already the contours of the face are fluctuating, the features hazing over, the hair dissolving into a halo of melting gold. The light spreads out in immense curves ranging from bright yellow to purple, and finally shading off little by little into a pale blue which in turn merges with the dark blue of the night.[18]

This is a resurrected Christ like one has never seen. This is not the Pantocrator, severe as he rules eternally. Nor is this the instructing Christ of the resurrection appearances, the serene Christ of the Ascension scenes, or Christ in kingly triumph over the forces of death and evil. Huysmans refers to the "smiling majesty" of Grunewald's figure,[19] though this requires some qualification. The face is radiant with joy but perhaps more with kindness as the eyes penetrate the onlooker. The face is radiant both in color and demeanor. One might conclude that Grunewald's risen Christ is a mystical portrayal, and that would be accurate if "mystical" is not equated with otherworldly indifference. That is, while there is a sense of otherness created by its emphasis on light, the painting highlights the beautiful flesh of the risen Christ. While robes do drape his form, much of his body is still in view: in addition to his face most of both arms, half his torso, and a great deal of his legs are exposed. The wounds in the palms, the feet, and side are evident but otherwise this is transformed flesh. The Christ who has known the depths of human affliction has also

---

[18]Ibid., 15.
[19]Ibid.

known the transforming resurrection power of the Holy One. And yet even this marvelously transformed resurrected Christ holding his arms wide, cruciform-like, reminds the viewer of the suffering this transformed Christ has known.

Grunewald's juxtaposition of grotesque crucifixion and radiant, mystical resurrection suggests that the message of God's shared experience of suffering with people in pain is accompanied by a message that God who resurrects the dead can transform suffering. That is, not only can people persevere; they can discover hope again sometimes in unexpected, resurrection ways.

We have to be very careful, even cautious with this counterpoint, for one too easily speaks the resurrection message as the panacea to suffering. Theologically the crucifixion and the resurrection stand in tension, and correlatively despair and hope may live in long-standing tension for the person afflicted. The "meantime" may last a very long time, even the duration of one's life. In the world of our God there are no cure-alls or timetables, and the mystery of this world and God's way are beyond precise description or understanding. That does not get God or anyone off the hook; but that is part of the reality with which we contend. Still, the proclamation of the gospel must include words of hope for transformation. A preacher who is sensitive to the meaning of the gospel and people's lives will work sensitively with this Good News, not setting forth illusions or false expectations. At the same time the preacher is not limited only to the confession that "God and God's people are hurting with you."

The latter part of the previous statement gets at important dimensions of resurrection's power. God's people need to be moved to action in behalf of people in pain. They need to be actively engaged to break the bonds of death and roll back the stones which imprison others. The proclamation of resurrection is a call for active care in behalf of those in pain. God's people can effect transformation. Thus worshiping the God of pathos and resurrection power pushes God's people to become what they ought to be—a community of mutual support.

Mutual Support of the Faith Community

The inability of so many people to comprehend the intersections between their own experiences and other people's experiences contributes largely to the absence of mutual support in the community of faith. The New Testament assumes that mutual support is a given among God's people (e.g., Acts 4:32-35), but all too often isolation and formal, superficial relationships are the experience of many people in a congregation.

The Church ought to be a primary context which encourages habitual patterns of attitudes and behavior which are attentive to the pain of other persons. What the Church ought not encourage are friends like those Job had to endure: all answers and little care. The Church as *koinonia* is a context in which persons in pain can find and experience mutual support. There they find persons who represent the pathos and care of the Holy One encountered in worship together. Preaching needs to encourage and help to cultivate attitudes and behavior consistent with the *koinonia* nature of the body: e.g. honest and patient sensitivity, dogged loyalty, and a sense of interconnectedness.

Preaching must endeavor to counteract the privatization of faith and the trend toward congregations which more closely resemble club membership than family membership. Preaching which attends to pain must differ from that preaching which views saving souls, not worship, as the objective of preaching. This utilitarian revivalism cares most about numerical results; preaching is for conversion as everything else retreats in the path of this weekly revivalist blitzkrieg. Preaching that touches pain must also differ from the lecture type of sermon which sets out to solve a social problem or offer a stimulating discourse on a theological issue. Nor should preachers delude themselves into believing that therapeutic sermons which emphasize "getting in touch with our feelings" and have no reference to the Holy One are anything but more than group therapy in the sanctuary. Finally, preaching to pain must differ from that worship which is more interested in performance and aesthetic beauty than substance. Fill in the cracks of most other religious gatherings, and it is much the same: numbers, issues, problems, feelings, performances. What they are missing are real persons and relationships, the stuff of which faith, the Church, human life, and God are about. Only if persons are the mission of the congregation will that congregation take suffering seriously. Numbers, issues, problems, feelings and performances do not suffer; persons with unique personalities and needs do.

The experience of the community's mutual support in historic African American churches is instructive for the way a congregation ought to attend to suffering persons. As James Cone describes this faith tradition,

> It appears that slaves are not troubled by the problem of evil in its academic guise; they know intuitively that nothing will be solved through a debate on that problem. They deal with the world as it is, not as it might have been if God had acted "justly." They attend to the present realities of despair and loneliness that disrupt the community of faith. The faithful seem to have lost faith, and the brother or sister experiences the agony of being alone in a world of hardship and pain.
>
> I couldn't hear nobody pray,
> Oh, I couldn't hear nobody pray.
> Oh, way down yonder by myself,
> And I couldn't hear nobody pray.
>
> Thus it is the loss of community that constitutes the major burden. Suffering is not too much to bear, if there are brothers and sisters to go down in the valley to pray with you.[20]

Likewise, in the tradition of many African American churches, communicating the pathos and resurrection power of God is not only proclaiming proper images of God, but also the presence and intentions with which the sermon is delivered to the people. It may be useful, for instance, for the preacher in the moments of meditation before the sermon to imagine the particular congregation in the arms of God, like a loving parent holding her children close. The intention here is neither to be sentimental nor psyche up the preacher, but to help the preacher comprehend the *holy* context of proclamation. It is not too much to claim that the preacher needs to experience the pathos of God in order to communicate it to the congregation. Words and creative turn-of-phrase alone cannot communicate the heart of the message; the

---

[20]James Cone, *The Spirituals and the Blues, An Interpretation* (New York: Seabury Press, 1972) 64.

presence of the proclaimer must undergird the sermon's verbal content. This concern is, of course, very slippery for purposes of definition. The point is that pathos by definition has a visceral dimension. The rationality and aesthetic pleasure of words cannot communicate the heart of God; God's pathos must be embodied.

By the same token pain is not a rational category; it is felt. Yet too much of our preaching about suffering seems to be aimed primarily at the minds of our hearers. We try to explain God's ways (theodicies): laying blame on fallen humanity, or the devil, or perhaps indirectly on God's providence to explain the matter. Even the most pastoral of situations, the funeral, seems too often more bent on explaining than communicating the caring presence of God and the faith community: "She's better off where she is; God had a reason for calling her home." Intentions may be to console, but the result, even if immediately unrecognized by the bereaved, is a denial of their real pain.

In its overall effect the sermon ought to speak to more than the congregation's minds; their viscera should be engaged as well. I use the term "viscera" in distinction from the more limited term "emotions," for the latter tends to be associated with a narrower range of human experience and is often more concerned with effect than content. Emotional preaching does have a sorry history of manipulation as the emotional *means* have been tools to accomplished prescribed *ends*. Our concern here is that the preacher will be able to communicate the pathos of God's being and presence only as the words which describe that pathos have more than their cognitive associations behind them. This is why the use of narrative, both biblical and experiential ones, can be so useful. Narratives are self-involving. Flesh and blood stories, not cardboard character illustrations, intersect with the lives of the congregation.

Those intersections can become the basis on which mutual support in the community of faith begins and is sustained. This mutual support should not be underestimated in its importance. For many persons in pain that mutual support is no add-on to their faith experience; it may be the only thing which helps them to hang on. In this respect we would do well to appreciate and recover a dimension of worship prominent in Hebrew Scripture: the prayer of lament. As the previous chapter observed, the sermon can function in much the same way as the lament: identifying (and even complaining about) sources of pain, recalling God's care in past difficulties, and expressing hope for God's present and future care. It is not only the formal function of lament which is important but its contextual function as well; for these brutally honest and hopeful expressions to God took place in the context of the covenant community. Samuel E. Balentine notes the contrast between this *community* context of worship and the isolation represented by the fatalistic musings of the writer of Ecclesiastes.

> In the Psalms it is a problem confronted within the sphere of the cult and with the support of the cultic community. When questions about the meaning of life are asked in this atmosphere, even when they reflect a note of uncertainty and despair, they remain essentially questions directed toward God. As such they can be channelled into an experience of worship which provides the suppliant with resources sufficient to keep the uncertainty from lapsing into despairing skepticism.[21]

The opposite, the threat, to passionate faith is despair, giving up. The community of mutual support may be the most effective deterrent to this loss of relationship with God, for even if God is hidden, even if God seems cruel or uncaring, the real arms of persons in the community of faith are there to lean on. For those clinging to meaning only by their fingernails, the strong arms of fellow believers who care out of their shared experiences of joy and sorrow can be the difference between faith with a glimmer of hope and despair. The dangers of isolation and abandonment are far more threatening to faith than doubts, anger, or pointed questions. As the laments of Scripture express, the negative feelings can be offered to God in prayer. Like a strained friendship, as long as there is some communication, there is some hope. When communication stops, there is isolation which leads to giving up (despair) and ultimately to the loss of relationship.

---

[21]Samuel E. Balentine, *The Hidden God: The Hiding of the Face of God in the Old Testament* (Oxford: Oxford University, 1983) 169.

Geoffrey Wainwright has listed eight "moods and attitudes characteristic of Christian worship [which] express the multiple aspects of the personal relationship, both dynamic and purposive, between God and humanity which is entailed in the making of humanity in the divine image." The first six are very familiar: adoration, confession of sin, proclamation and thanksgiving, commitment, intercession and expectation. The last two may sound peculiar to some ears, and Wainwright notes that these "two moods or attitudes . . . are less characteristic of the public liturgy of the church," finding their primary expression "in an individual's more private experience with God." These are the moods or attitudes of absence [of God] and wrestling [with God].[22]

It is curious that these two moods which are associated with suffering have been exiled to the sphere of private piety. It is more than curious; it is tragic, for by limiting these expressions to the private devotional life, the necessary connection between the community of mutual support and the individual's own faith journey through and with pain are excluded except in "practical ways." That is, the solidarity which could be gained and which is sorely needed by individuals in pain comes about in extra-worship contacts. The opportunity for complaint, anger, feelings of god-forsakenness, and wrestling with God are systematically excluded from the community's worship. Thereby is excluded solidarity in suffering through a corporate encounter with the Holy One who knows that suffering. How then do we cultivate this solidarity and thereby help persons, including ourselves, in times of affliction?

Building on Weil's categories, Dorothee Soelle states that the threat of afflictive suffering to faith is that one will remain "mute and numb" in the wake of that suffering, suffering she describes as that which "strikes us blind and deaf and leaves us mutilated." The loss of passion by affliction means that "even joy and happiness can no longer be experienced intensely." The silence before suffering thus becomes the groundwork for life without passion, apathy. "If people cannot speak about their affliction they

---

[22]Wainwright, *Doxology*, 37-44.

will be destroyed by it, or swallowed up by apathy."[23]

The task for the community of faith becomes solidarity with the afflicted, and that solidarity is possible only if others in the community can experience the connections between their suffering and others' suffering. Though they may not have known affliction, they are capable of recalling more than the cognitive dimensions of their struggle with pain. Only a faith which is rooted in the whole person—mind, heart, soul, and strength—can have this sort of passionate care, this solidarity with the afflicted to which the community of faith is called. The New Testament describes this in terms of *koinonia*. Every dimension of the community's experience together was shared in mutual support (e.g., Acts 2). They took action when there was need.

What has so often been absent from worship is a sense that this mutual support draws on the common experience of the pain of God, the pain of the members of the faith community, and the pain of each worshiper. As the afflicted have the opportunity to hear their pain articulated and offered to God in preaching, they do so in the presence of the God who knows, not knows about, their pain. They do so in the presence of fellow believers who discover that their experiences of pain and their experiences of care by God and members of the faith community must now be brought to their relationship with afflicted brothers and sisters. With this mutual support each person in the faith community may recognize that she or he is not alone. The resulting care and attentiveness to the needs of the afflicted will not solve their problems, for affliction—because it involves persons—is rarely "fixed" just like that. Perhaps healing can begin, or at least the slide into indifference and apathy can be checked by hope in the care of God and fellow believers.

So how does preaching aid in this process? We hope that the following sermons illustrate how these emphases of the pathos and resurrection power of God, the mutual support of the community of faith, and the passionate faith journey of the whole person can be held before the congregation as part of the vision

---

[23]Soelle, *Suffering*, 2, 39, 76.

of God's Kingdom. There is a teaching function to preaching which is crucial, for over a period of time the folk in the pew will become familiar with, and even live out of these important emphases of the vision of God's Kingdom. They should hear them in prayer and proclamation, in song[24] and confession, in greeting and benediction; and these grand dimensions of the Kingdom will become part of their mind, heart, soul, and strength.

Still, proclamation is not primarily about teaching; it is an opportunity to help worshipers encounter the Holy One. The preacher would do well to introduce the congregation to the variety of testimonies in scripture which give witness to the pathos and resurrection power of God, the community of mutual support, and the passionate faith journey of the whole person. The preacher would do well to help the congregation see and feel the connections between their own experiences and experiences of persons and nations beyond their immediate context. Thus it is arbitrary and illusory to preach some sermons which deal with personal issues and other sermons which deal with social issues, or to differentiate doctrinal sermons from experiential ones. These are false distinctions which isolate certain forms of pain from other forms of pain and certain suffering folk from other suffering folk.

The point of the preaching advocated here is to point the congregation to the Holy One who is known by pathos and resurrection power, who calls the community of faith to care for one another in mutual support, and who calls whole persons to a passionate journey of faith. If such preaching can help to shape those sorts of persons and communities, then we will have been tools of God's grace to cultivate holy people. For these holy people are the people of the Holy One, the Holy One who liberated Israel from the pain of slavery's oppression and who redeemed the world through the passionate life, death and resurrection of Jesus Christ.

---

[24]See David Nelson Duke, "Giving Voice to Suffering in Worship: A Study in the Theodicies of Hymnody," *Encounter* (Summer 1991) 263-72.

Epilogue

Throughout this chapter I have made an assumption which the reader may not have shared, but which I mention only now in order to raise a point. As I have spoken of pain, I have consciously had in mind the varieties of pain which afflict people: emotional, relational, economic, political, social, spiritual, and all the intersections among these forms. The reader would do well to engage in some self-examination: Was this essay heard as a discussion of personal pain without reference to its roots in social structures or vice versa? Preaching is often plagued with an either-or mentality on these matters. For some, pain is a matter of dealing with the varieties of social oppression; for others, a matter of personal crisis. Thereby some emphasize one or the other or try to give "equal time" over the course of the preaching year. We will not help to cultivate a community of mutual support nor understand the depth of God's care and work unless we break down these artificial distinctions.

—DND

Part Two

Practice:

Illustrative Sermons and Commentary

3

"Woman, Your Son"

John 19:25-27

Comment

We have spoken of the need for a certain reticence of speech when preaching to pain, the significance of what is not said sometimes outweighing the significance of what is. This sermon, on a particularly wrenching text and theme, seeks to make appropriate use of sermonic "silence." This happens literally in the recounting of the grief of Jesus' mother and his friend at Golgotha, at which point "we must turn our faces, for this grief is not ours to watch." It happens more importantly in the way our own griefs are alluded to with words that are simple and spare, language that describes far less than it evokes. Most of all this sermon works carefully not to overpromise a resolution of human grief, while pointing steadily to the real provision of community extended in this text. These various dimensions of reticence may not only honor the listener's circumstance and freedom, they may open up surprising space in which a measure of healing can occur.

The sermon itself was delivered as one of a series on "The Seven Words from the Cross," to a congregation like all congregations, replete with people whom the pastor knew to be scattered all along grief's very long road.

Have you ever thought what a difference it might make if Jesus were in the flesh with us, at least sometime? What if he walked on human feet again and were here for you; and you could gaze upon your hope in a face and hear it in a human voice? You could touch him if you like, just to make sure. You could ask him anything you may have been aching to ask for a long time. Some of us are so tired of not knowing what direction to take. Some of us are so tired of needing some assurance and not feeling it. Some of us are so hungry for hope. What if you could sit down across the table with his kind of wisdom, or take a long, quiet walk on a shaded path with him, or just once feel on your shoulder the touch of his strong hand? Would it not go a long way toward making us well and giving us heart for the journey?

Once on the earth there were people who had this gift. Most of them, of course, did not know what they had. Apparently a few of them at least sensed something of who he might be, and they drew great strength in keeping close to him. The Fourth Gospel, for instance, tells of one disciple whom Jesus especially loved and who dearly loved him. We often identify this "beloved disciple" with John, the son of Zebedee, because the Fourth Gospel comes to us with John's name on it; but the truth is, we are never told his name, and it is just as well. Whoever this young man was, he knew something. We always see him standing near Jesus. And on the last night at the Supper, we are told he leaned his tired and sorrowful head upon Jesus' breast. Can you imagine?

And there was another who loved him this much and even more. Who could have loved him more than she did? Mary, his mother, had held him for us all. Had cradled him in her arms and held him in her eyes. She had loved no sound in the world more than his laughter, and she hung on his words. When he was hers to hold, she would kiss his cuts and wipe his tears. And when he was older and still with her, she was on the fortunate receiving end of his touch and his word for whatever grieved her. Think of the treasure Mary had! And she needed it, as most mothers need their children, only more so. For she also knew something, had known it from the beginning—though the older she got, the more she must have wondered how much she really knew.

Someone has said that raising a child is the process of losing a child, and that was never truer of any parent than it was of Mary. When Jesus was twelve he disappeared one day. Mary searched and scrambled with Joseph to find him, and when they did, it was only to hear him say to his own parents that where he belonged was his Father's house. In a way, she spent the rest of her days trying to find him. More and more, he belonged not to her, but to the world and to God. And the worst of it, when he finally left home was not his physical absence, but that she could not keep hold of his mind and heart. How she wanted to understand him. If she could not hold her son anymore, she hungered at least to get her spirit around his spirit for a clear grasp of what he meant, especially what he meant for her. But more even than most sons and daughters elude their mothers and fathers, Jesus eluded her. Once she became so impatient she went out with her other sons to find him and bring him home. And when he would not come, did it not sting her heart to hear him say to that crowd of people she did not even know, "Here are my mother and brothers! Whoever does the will of God is my brother and my mother"? They took her home without him. Surely she cherished whatever moments he gave her. But what an aching hunger she must have had for more of Jesus with her.

Then came the end. Incomprehensible, unspeakably horrible, the news came: her son taken by soldiers, condemned to be executed, taken to be crucified. Sick at her stomach, trembling with fear, she makes her way through the streets. Her sister goes with her, along with some other speechless women and one young man with a grief-stricken face, the beloved disciple, who, like her, simply loved Jesus and wanted only to have him near. When they all arrived at the terrible place where three crosses stood and their unbelieving eyes took it in, how could human words tell the story of what died in them? A young man looks at his friend and teacher, his only hope in the world; a mother looks at her dear, dear son with nails through his hands and feet, and her heart is torn open with his suffering and with the bitter truth that she will never, ever, in any sense, hold him again. As she begins to weep we must turn our faces, for this grief is not ours to watch, though in a way it is our grief too.

Listen. All our grief has its place at the foot of that cross. Our grief over everyone we have loved who was taken from us, our grief over every crushed hope of getting it right, over every failure to keep what we wanted and needed, our grief over every frustrated longing to have the comforting face of God with us. You can do your weeping here—for all you love and cannot keep, for the face of perfect love you ache to see in your life but will not.

Jesus from his cross saw all this weeping. It is a grievous thing to see the ones you love in agony for you. Especially, I think, Jesus grieved for his mother. How could he watch her weep and his own heart not break? And just as surely as on that cross he was for-giving the world, he was forgiving her, too, for wanting him so much and understanding him so little. Even Saviors of the world must finally forgive their mothers and fathers.

Now he must speak to her. You might expect from him some word of comfort to his mother and his friend or some word of as-surance or of hope to make it easier to bear, but he says no such word. He says only this to his mother: "Woman, here is your son." And to his beloved disciple: "Here is your mother." That is all he said, and he never spoke a more tender word in his life.

For a man who is dying, it is a disarmingly practical word—seeing to it that a widow has provision and a home. Pure and sim-ple, Jesus is being a faithful son, not sentimentalizing over his mother but seeing to the particulars of her being cared for. How relentlessly mundane a Savior he always is. We keep hoisting him up into the clouds of love-in-the-abstract, making him a safe lit-tle holy man who stirs up spiritual feelings in us like "good will." But Jesus never peddled good will; he traded in love, which is al-ways stubbornly specific, personal, and concrete. "You take care of my mother. You feed that hungry child, find that man a job, speak the gospel to that lonely, lost woman there." His is a love you do. Even when he finds you in tears he gives you a love to do, just the way he did love in his dying. Have you caught the pattern of his first three words from the cross? With racking pain in his body and the crushing weight of the world on his soul, he still sees the people there and proceeds to extend to everybody on that hill what they need— prays forgiveness for the ones who are killing him, offers Paradise to another who is dying, and makes a home for his mother. That is how he wins the heart of the world—one specific, needy heart at a time.

But Jesus is giving more here than a home to his mother. He is answering the grief of his mother and of his disciple by giving these two grieving people to each other. Think of it as his last be-quest to them. Had Jesus been able to draw up a last will and tes-tament for his mother and his friend, what could he leave to them? He had no money, no house, no books. The only material thing he owned in the world was one finespun robe that had just been taken in a game of dice by a loudly laughing young soldier. All Jesus had now was his mother and his friend. What each of them wanted more than anything from him was for him to stay. What he gave them was each other. "Mother, I bequeath to you my friend to be your son. Friend, I bequeath to you this woman, to be your mother."

Remember he had said to his friends in the upper room, "I will not leave you orphans." He was telling them that his comforting Spirit would find them. But how would he do that when he was dead and gone? He starts it even as he dies by saying to the two who fear the most being left orphaned and grieving in the world, "Mother, I do not leave you desolate; I am giving you this man, my friend, to live with you in my place as your son. Friend, I do not leave you an orphan; I am giving you this woman, my mother, to live with you in my place as your comforter." And this is neither a game of pretending nor a second best. A miracle is taking place here, and a great grace is being given from the cross. Somehow a woman's grief is transformed into birthing a new child; and a young man's grief is touched and changed into his being born into a new family.

Do you see what it means? The Son of God on his cross not only receives and transforms the sin of the world into forgiveness and freedom, he receives and transforms the grief of the world into the beginnings of new family. All those for whom he dies he gives into one another's keeping. His gift for all our grief—our grief over the people who are gone from us and the dreams that have died for us and especially our grief that he seems far from us—is to make of all us orphans his own new family for one another and for the world.

Do not think that this lifts away all our grief. Mary's heart on that day, as old Simeon had said it would, was pierced with a sword; and such wounds as that a person carries with them always. But she walked away from her son's death leaning on the shoulder of a young man also wounded; and in the leaning was a kinship that was the perfect gift of God. In the leaning was love, the very love of Christ for them, through them. And that love, in the end, is all we grieving people need to find our way home.

O people of God, bring your grief here and receive the best gift for any grief. Take one another. Love one another as Christ has loved us. Be tender in your care for each other, for everyone is wounded. And lift up your hearts together, for Christ has prom-

ised his own triumphant love will spring to life in our kinship—
and it has! And it will! This is his answer to all those who wish
he were visibly present for us. As it turns out, in the family of
grace, he is! So with the mother and the beloved disciple of Jesus,
could we walk from his cross together, weeping with each other
perhaps, leaning on each other certainly, most of all belonging to
each other and eager to find our fellow weepers in the world and
offer them this best of news: none of us need be orphans now. By
the grace of God, look around you. Behold your mothers and your
fathers, your sons and your daughters, your sisters and brothers
in Christ Jesus. Thanks be to God!

—*PDD*

4

Seeing God in Shadows and Light
Genesis 32:3-31

Comment

Is this a sermon on the nature of God who dwells in darkness, or is it a sermon on broken families and friendships? It is both, for the account of Jacob fearing his brother and wrestling his God concerns both, as does our own experience of ruined relationships. So the sermon explores the invariable connection between our alienation from each other and our sense of alienation from God. How can it be otherwise?

The method is narrative, the Genesis text weaving in and out of the sermon and supplying its structure. To bring the issue more sharply into flesh and blood, a contemporary narrative is laid beside the biblical narrative, the account of a ruptured friendship between two women. There is typically a temptation for preachers, especially in our culture, to wrap up such sermons too tidily, for the conclusion of the thing to go more or less riding into the sunset. But the text at hand has more than a little ambiguity for its ending, so the sermon must submit us to some open-endedness. As God's faithfulness is promised, we are sent back into real relationships, frought with mystery and decision. Kierkegaard's council holds true: faith must not seem easier in the sermon than in the living room.

The familiar saying is that "Rules are made to be broken." Too often it seems that the same thing can be said for personal relationships: "Relationships are made to be broken." But if those relationships have meant anything at all, we desire that reconciliation take place and that genuine relationship be restored.

That very general description could apply to all of our relationships: to friendship, to marriage, to family, to the community
of faith—and to our relationship to God. Often broken human relationships affect or perhaps are reflective of alienation from God.
It may sound strange, but that is the way it should be. We should
experience some alienation from God when we experience alienation from other persons, for at the core of our faith is the claim
that our relationship to God is never a totally private matter, but
tied to the social fabric of our experience.

If there ever was a relationship difficult to put back together,
it was that of Jacob and Esau. You remember these very different
brothers. Esau was the eldest, his father's favorite child, a strong,
outdoors man, certainly fit for any Marlboro Country billboard.
Jacob, the younger of the twins, was a crafty, streetwise young
man, the favorite of his mother. Esau was impetuous; Jacob was
deliberate. With the help of his mother, Jacob was able to take
advantage of his brother and acquire the blessing and inheri-
tance intended for Esau, the eldest son. What was surely a rocky
sibling relationship became life-threatening for Jacob, and he fled
his family household just ahead of Esau's drawn sword.

Many years pass, and it is time for Jacob to go back home. His
going home is not so much a change in his attitude towards Esau,
but it is difficulties with a father-in-law who can almost match
Jacob scheme for scheme. How will Esau respond to his home-
coming? We pick up the story in chapter 32 of Genesis:

> And Jacob sent messengers before him to Esau his brother . . . ,
> instructing them, "Thus you shall say to my lord Esau: Thus says
> your servant Jacob, 'I have sojourned with Laban, and stayed
> until now; and I have oxen, asses, flocks, menservants, and
> maidservants; and I have sent to tell my lord, in order that I may
> find favor in your sight'." (vv. 3-5)

Jacob is no fool. He is properly deferential, verbally bowing
and scraping, calling his own brother "my lord Esau" and providing a substantial peace offering. The story continues:

> And the messengers returned to Jacob, saying, "We came to your
> brother Esau, and he is coming to meet you, and four hundred
> men with him." Then Jacob was greatly afraid and distressed;
> and he divided the people that were with him, and the flocks and

herds and camels, into two companies, thinking, "If Esau comes
to the one company and destroys it, then the company which is
left will escape." (vv. 6-8)

Jacob's worst fears seem to be realized, for it appears that Esau
with his small army seems intent on finally getting revenge. But
Jacob always has an angle; he divides his company into two
groups, so that one may be able to escape while Esau's men are
slaughtering the other one. Then Jacob petitions God: "Deliver
me, I pray thee, from the hand of my brother, from the hand of
Esau, for I fear him, lest he come and slay us all, the mothers and
the children" (v.11). Leaving nothing to chance, Jacob arranges
the peace offering to provide a clever buffer against attack,
breaking up his livestock and their herders into several waves so
that Esau will encounter a series of Jacob's company before he
ever gets to Jacob. Maybe Esau might kill the first group, but as
wave after wave of valuable livestock are presented as gifts to
Esau, surely, thinks Jacob, Esau's anger could be mollified. Jacob's motives and plan are clearly stated, as he says, "I may ap-
pease him with the present that goes before me, and afterwards
I shall see his face; perhaps he will accept me" (v. 20).

Then comes the heavy part. Jacob sends every last one of his
company ahead, and he lies down next to the stream Jabbok, not
knowing what the new day will bring: confrontation? acceptance? battle? forgiveness? life? death? It was not a night for sleep,
but a night of struggle.

The same night he arose and took his two wives, his two maids,
and his eleven children, and crossed the ford of the Jabbok. He
took them and sent them across the stream, and likewise everything that he had. And Jacob was left alone; and a man wrestled
with him until the breaking of the day. When the man saw that
he did not prevail against Jacob, he touched the hollow of his
thigh; and Jacob's thigh was put out of joint as he wrestled with
him. Then he said, "Let me go, for the day is breaking." But Jacob said, "I will not let you go, unless you bless me." And he said
to him, "What is your name?" And he said, "Jacob." Then he said,
"Your name shall no more be called Jacob, but Israel, for you
have striven with God and with men, and have prevailed." Then
Jacob asked him, "Tell me, I pray, your name." But he said, "Why
is it that you ask my name?" And there he blessed him. So Jacob

called the name of the place Peniel, saying, "For I have seen God face to face, and yet my life is preserved." The sun rose upon him as he passed Penuel, limping because of his thigh. (vv. 22-31)

Jacob is everyone of us. Like him, we work very hard to control our lives so that matters come out as we would like them to come out. We have Plans A, B, and C for most every occasion. Sometimes they work, and sometimes they do not. We, too, as calculating and frail human beings like Jacob, offer prayers for God's deliverance: for God to protect us when it does not appear that we will ultimately be able to protect ourselves. Like Jacob, most of us at one time or the other must come back to deal with broken relationships. Desperately we try every angle we know, but it seems so hopeless. And like Jacob we, too, finally realize that these broken human relationships have something to do with God, that a struggle with God is necessary in the midst of our struggles with other persons. Appeasement rarely works; the issue must be faced personally.

It is interesting that the narrator of the story is imprecise about the one with whom Jacob wrestles. When the story is over, Jacob knows it was God. But the nebulous character of the opponent's identity may be the narrator's way of saying that Jacob struggled not only with God, but that Jacob's feelings about Esau were in the shadows of that struggle, also. The struggle with God had very much to do with his lifelong struggle with Esau. Jacob's old ways of dealing with his distorted relationship with his brother could not work; something new was required.

Jacob's struggle ends; there is pain (his hip is dislocated) and there is blessing. Reconciliation has a price. Jacob is not the same: he has a new name and a new gait. Reconciliation of this broken relationship could not mean life as usual.

Those who know anything about life, who have really lived, know that the currently popular saccharine views of life simply are not true. For example, there are those calling themselves Christians who claim that our problems will go away if we will just "have enough trust in God." Christianity has always gone astray when it looked for life in the skies, instead of in the eyes of brothers and sisters. Life, and life's relationships, include pain. To risk relationship is to risk pain.

Perhaps many of you can empathize with my friend Meg. She has spent most of her life enjoying a rich friendship with Tracy. Though they have lived in different regions of the country for almost a decade, they have until recently kept up with each other through letters, phone calls, and visits. The two of them, especially Meg, have worked at sustaining that relationship. But recently something has happened, though it is hard to put a finger on exactly what happened. There was no crisis, just a general and gradual deterioration of their relationship. It has been like a knitted sweater unravelling. The loose thread began about a year ago, and through increasing neglect of the flaw, the garment has come apart to the point that it is all but unrecognizable and useless. It was a relationship lost through neglect, especially on Tracy's part. Her letters stopped; the phone calls were rare; the visits nonexistent. Meg is frustrated, angry, and hurt. She has depended on that relationship with Tracy for years, and now only something superficial remains. She is at her wit's end as to how to repair her friendship with Tracy.

Not surprisingly, Meg's deteriorating relationship with Tracy has been accompanied by a sense of inadequacy in her relationship with God. Worship seems empty, prayer fruitless, and the church absurd. What is she to do? Smile and hope the problem will go away? She wants so desperately to remain strong in her faith, but how does she find hope in the midst of her sense of abandonment and loneliness—both from God and one of the most important human relationships in her life?

Meg is having *her* struggle at the stream Jabbok. She is not always sure with whom or what she is struggling, but she knows it has something to do with God, with her friend Tracy, and with the integrity of her own faith. The honest prayer of the psalmist could be her prayer as well.

O Lord, my God, I call for help by day;
 I cry out in the night before thee.
Let my prayer come before thee,
 incline thy ear to my cry!
For my soul is full of troubles,
 and my life draws near to Sheol.
 . . .
Thou hast caused my companions to shun me;

> thou hast made me a thing of horror to them.
> I am shut in so that I cannot escape;
>   my eye grows dim through sorrow.
> Every day I call upon thee, O Lord;
>   I spread out my hands to thee.   (Psalm 88:1-3, 8-9)

Note that the psalmist is praying to God, even though God's face seems to be hidden in the shadows. And yet the person prays. In anger, in frustration, this believer prays. The supplicant has prayed when God could be seen in the clear light of beauty and health, and now prays when God seems hidden in the shadows and all companions have abandoned him.

Like the psalmist and like Jacob, Meg in desperation is clinging to God, struggling with God, asking for a blessing. I can't tell you the end of her story, for it is not over. My hunch is it will turn out somewhat like Jacob's. Meg will not emerge unscathed. There will be pain, for in our encounter with God and real life relationships, that is the way it is. Until we live in the pure light of God's presence, questions about God and difficulties in human relationships will be a part of our experience.

One interesting repetition in the story of Jacob's struggle may be useful; the word "face" keeps showing up again and again. Jacob anticipates that his gifts of appeasement will allow him to see Esau's face and that Esau will accept him (v. 20). Jacob names the place of his struggle Peniel, because, he says, "I have seen God face to face, and yet my life is preserved" (v. 30). In the subsequent meeting of Jacob and Esau their reconciliation is described by Jacob: "for truly to see your face is like seeing the face of God, with such favor you received me" (33:10). By encountering the face of God in the shadows of his struggle, Jacob had come to understand the true face of Esau, and his own face, one who would no longer be known as Jacob, the grasping one, but Israel, one who strives with God.

We have often associated the face of God with light, and that is proper. Most paintings surround the figure of God with light, for light signifies transcendence, truth, purity, and holiness. But that must not be the only way we understand God, and Scripture makes this abundantly clear. God is present in life's shadows as well, in ways beyond our comprehension. That is the truth of the gospel: we see God in the shadows of the cross and in the light of the new dawn of resurrection. God is seen in shadows and light: in all of life, in all relationships, healthy ones and broken ones. There are no guarantees that the shadows will disappear, that broken relationships will all be healed. Again, Jacob's story is instructive, for it does not have a perfectly neat and happy ending. While Esau is quite accepting of Jacob, there continues to be some mistrust on Jacob's part, even in the face of Esau's affectionate welcome. Jacob continues to call his brother "my lord," and he will not turn his back on Esau. Jacob still is not sure if Esau's absence-of-malice is real. A real scar remains in Jacob's soul despite the promising reconciliation with his brother.

Finally there is the practical question for our faith: How do we avoid a total paralysis of faith when we find ourselves primarily in the shadows of broken relationships? Part of the problem with that question is that it may assume that we have to have it all together to be bearers of the gospel, that we must always embody solid relationships to promote the whole relationships brought by the Good News. We would do better to use the image suggested by Henri Nouwen, "the wounded healer." We can be wounded healers. This is our role as Christians: to be no more and no less than wounded healers. We can be wounded and yet through the mystery of God's grace bring healing to an alienated world, an alienation in which we participate.

Some of you may be familiar with Graham Greene's novel *The Power and the Glory,* the story of a character known as the Whiskey Priest. This priest drinks too much, fathers an illegitimate child, and loses any personal sense of God in his life. Though he believes his own prayers to be ineffectual and his priestly acts to be mortal sin for himself, he continues his priestly functions of hearing confession, baptizing children, saying Mass, and giving moral instruction—in a country which has banned the church and branded all priests criminals. Living on the run and fearing for his life, the Whiskey Priest continues to fulfill his priestly duties, and somehow God uses his messed up life to bring grace to other people. God was at work in the shadows and the light.

When the newly called disciples asked Jesus where he lived, Jesus simply said, "Come and see." And during the next three years, they did see: Jesus lived with all persons, especially those rejected by his society. If you have risked significant relationship with another human being, you have probably known what it means to be rejected at some level. Christ still lives among the rejected.

We live in health and sickness; we live in healthy relationships and sick relationships; we live in light and shadows. Like the disciples, we and those around us ask, "Where is God in all of this?" May we, as Christ's followers, respond as our Master and say, "Come and see." For by the grace known in Christ, God will be seen in light and shadows.

—DND

5

The Tree, the Cave, and Beyond

1 Kings 19:1-18

Comment

Like a fresh baked cake and a jar of water in the wilderness, the retelling of this ancient story can be an empowering nourishment for the depressed and despairing. This text "feeds" the wounded, feeds by its utter simplicity in some respects ("Get up and eat") and also by its impenetrable mysteries (the Silence itself posing unanswerable questions). The text also "leads" the wounded— moves us with Elijah from isolation to lament to community. The only way to botch this text homiletically is to do anything with it other than tell the story.

So the structure of the sermon simply unfolds according to the structure of the narrative. The introduction is a very deliberate example of the "Gathering" function of preaching. With quick strokes, lighthearted at first, a circle is drawn large enough to include everyone in the room. Still, the sermon recognizes, especially in the conclusion, that listeners will be found by this text at more than one place: at the Tree, in the Cave, on their way to or from. The final image of walking down a road points pastor and congregation past the sermon and invites the taking of real steps.

Anybody here depressed? Anybody here worn out with what you do, burned out, stressed out, tired of trying, ready to resign something, throw in the towel and quit?

Have I got a story for you.

Some of you aren't down at all. But life being what it is, you and I being what we are, the day will likely come—count on this— when you do your sighing and weeping and want to do your quitting. If this story doesn't have your name on it now, sooner or later it will. I hope you'll remember.

There are times when it seems to me everyone I know is struggling. A veteran minister friend tells me he sees more people now who are bottomed out, burned out, and depressed than he has ever seen before. "What's going on?" he said. I couldn't say; I just knew what he meant.

Here's a picture in our text of a gifted, strong, fairly faithful human being, slumped down under a broom tree with his head in his hands. And there are times looking out at this congregation when I think what I see is a forest of broom trees, an exhausted individual slumped under each one.

Have you come to church or have you come about a day's journey into the desert? Sit here for awhile under your tree of disappointments. There was a day when this man Elijah was standing, standing tall by an altar. On that day he told all the people "Come closer" to see the power of the living God. Today he does not have the heart to say this, but I will. Come closer to him now. There is plenty to be seen of God here too.

Pay close attention to the kind of person this is who is so discouraged he wants to die. Is he a failure? No. Has he been unfaithful? No. Would you call him weak? No one could be stronger or healthier. Discouragement does not have to be a sign that you are sick; it can be a sign that the systems you care about are sick. What happens to healthy, caring people when they are put in sick institutions, sick families, sick circumstances? As Walker Percy put it: "[Is] the Self . . . Depressed because there is something wrong with it or [is] Depression a Normal Response to a Deranged World"?[1] If there is any health in you at all, if you care about anything that matters, you are a candidate. You will bear in your body the burden of the sickness around you.

Elijah loved his country but his country was sick. His people were intoxicated with stupid, cheap, feel-good religion. His king was a hollow man. His queen was cruel and coming after him. He bore the weight of all that disease in his body and soul. It gets inside you if you care. If you don't care it rolls off your back and you

---

[1]Walker Percy, *Lost in the Cosmos: The Last Self-Help Book* (New York: Farrar, Straus & Giroux, 1983) 73.

get to keep whistling. But everyone I know who tries to make a difference, everyone I know who ever made a difference has done his or her time under that tree.

Of course, it is usually hidden. The struggle is usually a secret. So most of us think we are the only ones. I'll bet some of you think there's something uniquely wrong with you— everybody else is brave and sure; you're the only one struggling with discouragement and doubt. If you could get inside your heroes you'd know better. When you see Elijah slouched under his tree with his head in his hands, you're not just seeing his bad day after his good day. You're seeing inside him, the hidden struggle beneath the outer success, the secret fear behind the public courage. Just like you. Just like me.

And he says "It is enough." This is the Crisis of the Tree. It is the crisis of exhaustion. It is enough—the word in Hebrew means *long*—long, long road; Lord, how long? "Enough. Let me die. I am no better than my ancestors." So depression leaves us with no sense of worth, and reduces us to measuring ourselves by everybody else: I'm worse than she is, better than he is, worse than he is. Elijah measures himself. "I'm no better than my fathers." Depressed or not, isn't this just like a man?—keeping score in some kind of competition with his fathers!

What does such a person need? He needs a great many things, but the first thing he needs is a nap.

To be a better saint you must be a better animal. You are not a spirit, you are a body. You rest. Sleep is grace. Sleep is trust. Sleep is obedience to the facts that you are not a god but a creature. Sleep is rehearsal for dying before being raised to new life. In Mendelsohnn's *Elijah* there is a wonderful pause in the story here. The choir breaks in to sing from the Psalm: "Thy Keeper will never slumber. He watching over Israel slumbers not nor sleeps." The eyes of God's love never close; you can close your eyes and sleep.

You can also eat. Elijah wakes up and smells pancakes. And there's a cup of cool water, and a stranger beside him saying, "How about some breakfast?" This is the kind of God we have: first things first! Nourish the body, be a creature, open your mouth and take your daily bread. Elijah does. Then he rolls over and goes back to sleep. So the angel wakes him again and feeds him again.

These recoveries take time.

But now when the angel feeds him there is mention of a pilgrimage. "Rise and eat, or the journey will be too great for you." "Journey?" says Elijah. "Journey? Didn't I just run a hundred and thirty miles? I'm all journeyed out! Don't tell me there's more!"

Yes. But here is the difference. You came here to escape something. Leave here to meet something. You were driven. Now be drawn. You were a fugitive. Now be a pilgrim. It's so much less exhausting.

So Elijah gets up and journeys forty days and nights to the holiest place he knows. Here the Bible calls it Horeb, elsewhere Sinai, the same mountain. The mountain that quaked and blasted and burned when God gave the Law to Moses. The mountain where Moses hid in a cave and saw God pass by. The mountain where Moses heard a Voice. Depressed and depleted, Elijah does a very human thing and a deeply wise thing. He goes back to what his past tells him is a likely place to be met by the living God. He goes to this mountain, and he enters a cave, crawls back into the womb and waits in the dark for God to speak.

And God speaks. Only it is not an encouraging word, not a welcome or a blessing—but a question. "What are you doing here, Elijah?" The God of Scripture is always asking questions. Those who go to God with questions are often met with new questions, God's questions. Elijah, what are you doing here?

Suppose you are discouraged. And suppose like Elijah you find yourself going back to some holy ground to find your bearings, to listen for a new word. Where would you go? What would constitute your cave? What if you went into your room, closed the door and got on your knees? What if you opened your Bible again? What if you literally went away to another place, a quiet place of retreat? Or what if, having long stayed away from church, you decided to return here to listen for a word? But imagine coming to church or to retreat or opening your Bible or getting on your knees—and being stopped by the question: What are you doing here? Are you looking for a feeling? Are you here for a quick fix? Have you come hoping to get something on your own terms? Do you have any idea whose name you are calling? What are you doing here?

Elijah is here for some pity. He has come to the cave for comfort. He is lonely, angry, tired—and knows how to pray. He does not fold his hands and "make nice," he pours out his sickness. His praying is wretching. "*I* fought for you, *they* killed your prophets. *I, I* alone am left and *they* seek *my* life." This is the grammar of discouragement. It's what we sound like when the sickness gets inside us. Prayer is getting it out.

What happens next is spectacular and disappointing. Everything happens that Elijah could hope for, everything that happened for Moses—a Wind ripping boulders off the mountain, an Earthquake, Fire. But these wonders are all empty. God is absent from them. Elijah has a Rocky Mountain view, hears the Hallelujah Chorus, and sees fireworks to boot—and feels nothing. This is the Crisis of the Cave. It is the crisis of silence.

When I was a teenager my family went every summer to the beach. Each year I would go out alone one night to sit before the sea. Watching it, hearing it, smelling it, seeing the stars, feeling the breeze in my face, there was no place on earth I felt closer to God. I will never forget the year I went back and sat where I had sat before, and felt nothing. And I waited and I prayed and I waited . . . nothing. C. S. Lewis said the one prayer God is likely never to answer is the prayer that says "Encore!"[2]

Go back to the holiest place you know, do all you have done before to invite the Voice. But be prepared for this: it may not be as it once was. Maybe all that will finally speak to you is how silent that place has become.

But guess what? Sometimes the silence itself has something to say. An empty experience can be a cradle for a new kind of word. Did Elijah hear "a still, small voice"? The Hebrew says he heard "a sound of thin silence."[3] The silence carried a word from God. Has God gone silent on you? Listen again. God's silence can speak.

The new word to Elijah had two parts: a Purpose Word and a Community Word. The Purpose Word was: Here's new work for

---

[2]C. S. Lewis, *Letters to Malcolm, Chiefly on Prayer* (New York: Harcourt & Brace, 1964) 27.

[3]John Gray, *I & II Kings: A Commentary,* The Old Testament Library (Philadelphia: Westminster Press, 1970) 406.

you. Get into politics, Elijah. Go be subversive in your world, anoint new kings, empower a new kind of government; empower your own successor too. How does God answer when you're small and circling yourself? A purpose bigger than the size of your self! If a terrible silence has come to your life, maybe the silence is a sign of a bigger mission than you have been serving.

Maybe it's also a sign that it is time to find your people. This was God's Community Word. God says: Oh, and Elijah? Mr. Everybody-Hates-Me I-I-I-Eli-I-jah? When you leave this cave of yourself and go blinking into the sunlight back home, please notice about 7,000 who are my faithful children and your sustaining family. You miscounted your community, Elijah, by 6,999.[4] The world is terrible, but not as terrible as you think. Let me introduce you to your family. Beware of staring too long at your wound. Go inside your private cave when you need to. But remember that the cave is not campground. It is a womb for birthing you out again into your purpose and into your family.

So where does this word find you? If it finds you under some tree of sorrow, you can weep and you can rest. If it finds you inside your cave of silence, you can be born outward to a new sense of your purpose and your people. Wherever this word finds you, it does not find you far from Christ—who also wept on a tree, and was laid in a cave, and who is risen to gather us to a purpose and a family.

Like him, Elijah got past his tree and his cave. I do not know how quick his step may have been or how high he held his head when he finally emerged. But he was walking toward his purpose now and toward his sisters and brothers. Somewhere down that road he found his joy. On that road, so will we.

—PDD

---

[4]Walter Brueggemann, *I Kings,* Knox Preaching Guides (Atlanta: John Knox Press, 1982) 90.

6

Called to Be Servants, Not Problem-Solvers

Mark 9:30-37; James 3:13-18

Comment

The text is a Pronouncement Saying, not an easy "form" from which to preach. Though Matthew and Luke offer the child saying in a different context from the servant saying, Mark combines them. The sermon does the same, interpreting one by the other, and drawing as well from the epistle lesson of the day.

Working with an image that is all too easily sentimentalized the sermon works deliberately both to desentimentalize and to make the proclamation plainly specific and concrete: What does Jesus' acted-out parable of holding a child suggest about embracing one's spouse or one's neighbor? What does it suggest about how we faithfully respond to the huge issues of world hunger or peacemaking? The text does not touch directly upon the congregation's pain, nor even the world's pain per se. Instead an alternative vision is offered of our central vocation as God's people in this world. As will be recalled, one gift a shepherd gives to the wounded is the gift of Leading, patiently pointing to God's vision of us and to our vocation with God. Fidelity to that vision and vocation is the beginning of healing for us and through us.

Picture yourself sitting in the yard, feeling the cool evening breeze, talking with friends; or sitting in front of a fire, talking about old times or times which may yet be. Inevitably those kinds of conversations come around to our ambitions for ourselves. We talk of what we hope to be doing in 10, 15, or 20 years; for others the look is backward, what we did 10, 15, or 20 years ago. And we share with friends what we hope we have accomplished or will accomplish. Those are special moments, moments in which we step outside of time.

Perhaps it was such an occasion when twelve young-to-middle-aged men began discussing their ambitions together. All twelve had recently walked away from their occupations to pursue another way of life. They wondered where this new way would take them: what power and prestige would they have in 10, 15, or 20 years? Would they be well known? Would they have a major impact on their country's future? Would they be important leaders? Which of them would achieve the most fame and power?

They were so busy considering these wonderful possibilities that they almost did not hear what their teacher said. What he said was hard to understand, though he had mentioned it before. For some reason he spoke of people trying to hurt him, that he would even be killed. Except he did not say it even that plainly. He said, "The Son of Man is to be betrayed into human hands, and they will kill him." These ambitious young men just did not understand him, and in their confusion they were afraid to ask for a clearer explanation.

The Teacher was just a little too pessimistic, they concluded. Sure, the odds might not be outstanding, but they were confident that they were backing a good risk. The Teacher had dropped just enough clues, and his miraculous wonders sealed the case: conclusion—the Teacher was the long-awaited Messiah. And it had been their good fortune that he had singled them out to be his specially chosen followers. Just think of it: they were part of the entourage of that Messiah who would restore their nation's political fortunes. A great time was ahead, and they would be in the thick of it! What special roles he must have in mind for them! But who would get the choicest positions? That was the debate at the moment. Would the Teacher choose the one with the most political savvy? the one with the most economic clout! the one with the most knowledge of the Law? the most charismatic leader? the best physical specimen? Who would be the greatest?

The conversation comes to an end as their day's journey is completed, and they settle in a house in the town of Capernaum. Then the Teacher asks them an embarrassing question, "What were you discussing on the way?" There is an awkward silence, and their silence gives them away. It is, as we say, one of those teachable moments, and Jesus of Nazareth makes the most of it.

> "If any one would be first, he must be last of all and servant of all." And he took a child, and put him in the midst of them; and taking him in his arms, he said to them, "Whoever welcomes one such child in my name welcomes me; and whoever welcomes me welcomes not me but the One who sent me."

Jesus once again turns the world upside down. He offers a new understanding of greatness.

Jesus brings a different standard to measure greatness. Greatness is measured not by success, but by service. Lest anyone miss his point, he acts out his claim; he hugs a child. Just hugs a child. Mark's description is helpful: Jesus speaks of the need for them also to "*receive* one such child." Receive means to welcome, not just to acknowledge, or to commend, but welcome with open arms. It is one thing to hug a child and then to get down to real business. It is quite another to do as Jesus does and make that embrace of the child *the* most important business in the world. Jesus was not being sentimental, pointing out how adorable kids are. Rather, he was trying to act out the nature of servanthood, a relationship in which another person is important only for the reason that he or she is that other person. Jesus is saying that other persons are embraced, not for what they offer us or for what we can make of them, but just because they are our brothers and sisters.

In hugging this child, Jesus was acting out a parable on the nature of servanthood, the servanthood to which he calls his disciples. Children are cute; but in their littleness and powerlessness they are insignificant in the arenas which the world considers important for greatness. One doesn't become well known by hugging a little child. One doesn't become wealthy by hugging a little child. One doesn't become influential in the halls of power by hugging a little child. Embracing the lowly, the weak, the helpless does not result in success or greatness as we most often define it.

Jesus' disciples were confused, and so are we. Jesus turns our values upside down. As one commentator notes, Jesus may be playing in the same ballpark, but he's playing a different kind of ballgame. The rules are not the same. His definition of greatness does not match with ours. He turns the world right side up.[1]

The Hebrew prophets, Amos, Hosea, Micah, and Jeremiah, had played by the same strange rules, and you remember their small following. They called God's people back to justice, not to some abstract notion of being just. Justice was concrete action. Justice, they said, meant simply caring for the orphans, for the widows, for the foreigners. Few responded to their pleas.

Few understood Jesus, and too often, few of us understand him either. We do understand the need for service, and we do make valiant efforts to be servants. Yet, too often, we understand no better than those disciples what Jesus was driving at. We really have not grasped the significance of his receiving the child, of hugging a child.

Much of the time most of us approach service as problem-solvers, not as servants. We determine a need—a problem, and then spend our energies sincerely trying to make things come out right. There is nothing immoral in that approach, but it really does not get at what Jesus meant when he called us to be servants who receive children, the helpless ones.

We problem-solvers must worry about accomplishments, about achieving goals. That is not bad in itself. But problem-solvers almost inevitably become absorbed in the task, rather than in the persons they wish to serve. Problem-solvers tend to regard other persons as problems to be solved, problems to be straightened out.

One of my classes was reading biographies of major religious thinkers. As we were discussing the life story of one individual, who was particularly serious about achieving sacrificial humility, one student asked a profound theological question. She said, "All this is fine, but did the guy enjoy ice cream with his friends?" Do we become so wrapped up in dealing with persons as problems that we cannot enjoy ice cream with them?

---

[1]Donald B. Kraybill, *The Upside-Down Kingdom* (Scottdale PA: Herald Press, 1978) 24.

What if we regarded other persons as mysteries rather than problems?[2] Does not service then take on a whole new perspective? Human beings are mysteries. Each person is unique, not easily translated into the equations which we can manipulate to solve problems. If we regarded other persons as mysteries, we would not try to impose on them our plans for changing them and then become frustrated when they fail to live up to our plans. We would not expect our spouses to become the embodiment of that so-called perfect husband or wife. How many marriages could be more loving if we could avoid the problem-solving approach which we impose on our mates? And what about our neighbors or workplace acquaintances? How much better could we relate to them if we regarded them as mysteries, not requiring that they fit into our mold of friendship. We could be friends.

Problem-solvers also worry about efficiency, and that is not all bad either. But efficiency requires measurable results, and human beings and human problems are not reducible to measurable results. Mother Teresa simply holds the hand of a dying leper woman in Calcutta. There is nothing efficient about that, but we recognize that Mother Teresa is a servant of God. She regards people as mysteries, not problems. Millard Fuller is very conscious of efficient house building, but his commitment to building decent housing for the poor is not based on some efficient understanding of the world. Fuller's Habitat for Humanity helps people construct decent houses because he regards all people as mysteries, people who have needs which cannot be met by traditional problem-solving methods. We recognize that Millard Fuller is a true servant of God. We wouldn't be surprised if Mother Theresa or Millard Fuller just took time to hug a child and spend the afternoon with that child, even if other work was pressing.

To regard other persons as mysteries, to cease regarding them as problems, means a renunciation of our desire to dominate. Problem-solvers have to be on top of the situation, literally on top. They must be in control. If nothing else, problem-solvers talk more than they listen. Servants listen. Over 40 years ago the Christian

---

[2]Cf. Craig Dykstra, *Vision and Character* (New York: Paulist Press, 1981) 36-40.

martyr, Dietrich Bonhoeffer observed that

> Many people are looking for an ear to listen. They do not find it among Christians, because these Christians are talking where they should be listening. But he who can no longer listen to his brother will soon be no longer listening to God; he will be doing nothing but prattle in the presence of God too. . . . in the end there is nothing left but spiritual chatter. . . .[3]

Jesus said, "Whoever wants to be first, must be last of all and servant of all." To regard other persons as mysteries and be servants is to let go of the need to dominate, even the need to talk; and simply to BE to the other person what we can best be. A servant receives, welcomes, holds out open arms.

Problem-solvers burn out on the tough issues. Did you ever notice how difficult it is to sustain interest, much less commitment to the struggle against hunger? Burnout comes easily. A very sincere man said to me, "I would quit eating steak if I thought it would make a real difference in world hunger." He meant it; that was no empty promise, but he could see no reasonable, efficient solution to hunger in sight. No, we shouldn't give up the hope that hunger can be significantly reduced, but we must not let our approach be strictly that of problem-solving. To be God's servants in the fact of increasing hunger means faithfully to do and be what we can be, searching always to regard and receive hungry persons as mysteries. Sometimes just holding the hands of the dying poor makes headlines and inspires others. Sometimes it doesn't. Whatever the results, our call as servants is to be faithful, grounding our service in love to God who was made known to us in the form of a servant. Servants don't calculate; servants love. The fundamental issue for the servant's faith is not what one accomplishes, but how one lives.

This contrast is evident in our reading from the Epistle of James. James contrasts "earthly" wisdom with wisdom which is of God. Earthly wisdom involves "jealousy," "selfish ambition," "boastfulness," and "falsehood." Earthly wisdom, says James, leads to disorder. James seems to be describing a kind of wisdom

---

[3]Dietrich Bonhoeffer, *Life Together,* trans. John W. Doberstein (New York: Harper & Row, 1954) 97-98.

which needs to dominate, to be on top, to solve problems. In contrast, wisdom of God is "pure," "peaceable," "gentle," "open to reason," and "without uncertainty and insincerity." The wisdom of God results in righteousness for it is "sown in peace by those who make peace." One is reminded of the slogan used by the Fellowship of Reconciliation: "There is no way to peace; peace is the way." For all their calculating, the centuries of problem-solvers seem to have moved no closer to peace in a world torn by violence. They—we—have chosen the path of dominance, of competing for power. Theirs—ours—is the earthly wisdom described by James, a wisdom of jealousy, selfish ambition, and boastfulness. Indeed the result has been disorder, as James writes.

All this is to say that Jesus and James, too, help us rethink our understanding of servanthood. Have we not too often pursued servanthood in personal self-establishment, working to make ourselves ready to serve? Jesus' hug of the child tells us that servanthood has more to do with relationships than with personal self-discipline. Servanthood is less a matter of working on ourselves than holding out our arms to others. Servanthood has less to do with me and most of all to do with us.

There is nothing idealistic or naive about being a servant. We must serve in the midst of our very complicated and unorganized lives. We must open our arms to others in the midst of the ups and downs in our own lives.

Some of you have seen the movie, *Tender Mercies*. The main character is Mack Sledge, a country-western singer whose life had almost reached the bottom; but while working for a sympathetic young widow and her son, he gets back on his feet. This story of Mack Sledge is a true-to-life representation of the struggles of servanthood. Mack and the young widow, Rosa Lee, eventually marry. They live a simple life, opening their arms to each other and other persons. Somehow Mack learns to treat people as mysteries, perhaps having learned from the mystery of his own mixed-up life. He tries to be a father to his young stepson, a boy who does not understand how and why his real Daddy died in Vietnam. He tries to relate to his grown daughter, whom he has not seen in eight years following the messy divorce from his former wife. He lives with the guilt of this lost opportunity of parenthood, with the memories of drunken abuse of his wife, with her resentment

of him now. He struggles to stay on the wagon, for alcoholism almost destroyed him. He struggles with his need to write music and
sing after a lost career; and as the film nears its end, he grieves
over the accidental death of his daughter. Having returned from
her funeral, he sulks and then angrily sobs to Rosa Lee, "I never
did trust happiness, and I never will." And yet, just after this grief-
filled outburst, he picks up a football, a football he had bought for
his stepson sometime during the funeral trip. The film ends with
Mack and the boy throwing an ordinary football. Just routine
play, but what an affirmation of life, community, and hope! Mack
Sledge's life had been full of hard knocks, but somehow in the
midst of extraordinary personal pain he still opens his arms to the
little child. This servant struggles, and so do we.

Strengthened by the ever-present love of God, God's servants,
with all their personal faults, live courageously, welcoming each
person into their lives with open arms, even as Jesus received the
child and embraced him.

Give what you have.

Give who you are.

That is the measure of greatness.

—DND

7

On Not Sulking through the Inevitable

Philippians 4:10-13

Comment

This sermon, based on a brief, much loved epistle text, chooses a very conventional structure. It's a dead ringer for three points and a big story! More accurately, it has a structure Fred Craddock would call: Not this, nor this, but this.[1] The movement in this structure, from Denial to Despair to Acceptance, does correspond to the zigzag road that most mourners find themselves walking.

Some of the various inadequate responses to human pain that were discussed in the opening chapters are here taken on outright: in particular, the several ways our piety has concocted to help us lie about our pain. The hope embodied in the sermon is that these need not be finally lies, but faltering steps on the way to the truth. The final word of the sermon points to both the pathos and the resurrection power we have urged throughout: the acknowledgment of loss and life, the actual acceptance of real loss and real life.

Back in the early years of this century a young woman was facing an ordeal. It's not important to know what her hardship was, but something was ahead of her that she could not change and did not wish to face. Fortunately she had a wise uncle who wrote her often. He was the famous and brilliant Baron Friedrich von Hügel, an Austrian Catholic theologian living in England. We still have his

---

[1]See Fred B. Craddock, *Preaching* (Nashville: Abingdon Press, 1985) 176-77.

letters to his niece, including a letter of encouragement as she
faces her ordeal. He reminds her that whether she endures these
weeks bitterly or nobly, "they will have to be got through. . . .
There they are." He says if she undergoes these weeks nobly and
seeks what is best, the time will pass and do her good, otherwise
the time will still pass but do her harm. He ends with these words:
"I now have come to feel that there is hardly anything more rad-
ically mean and deteriorating than, as it were, sulking through
the inevitable, and just simply counting the hours till it passes."[2]

Consider the phrase, "sulking through the inevitable." Does
it describe anyone of your acquaintance?

Here is a fact. For every one of us there come times or tasks
or circumstances that are not pleasant for us and that we cannot
change. There is a job to be done or a conflict to be faced or some
emotional wilderness to be worked through. And we would avoid
it if we could, but we cannot. There it is. It has to be gotten
through: the inevitable unpleasantness, inescapable drudgery or
conflict or grief. And Uncle von Hügel's letter says: "there is
hardly anything more . . . deteriorating than . . . sulking through
the inevitable."

Let us lay beside his letter another one. Here is another letter
of encouragement, oddly enough, written by someone locked away
in prison. An old missionary writes from the painful center of his
own inevitable unpleasantness, "I have learned in whatever condition I am to be content. I know how to be abased and I know how
to abound. In any and all circumstances I have learned the secret
of facing plenty and hunger, abundance and want. I am able to do
all things through the One who strengthens me."

Here is a man literally locked into his ordeal. He doesn't want
to be where he is. Imagine the daily horrors he may be facing:
cramped quarters, stench, darkness, manacles, rats, abusive
companions, stale bread, bodily discomfort, the mental agitation
of craving freedom and not having it. He'd leave if he could, but
he can't. And yet inside these iron limits, the old missionary isn't

---

[2]Baron Friedrich von Hügel, *Selected Letters*, cited in John Baillie,
A Diary of Daily Readings (New York: Charles Scribner's Sons, 1955)
162.

sulking. In fact he speaks of a contentment he's coming to find in this place, or in whatever place he may be.

Whatever place. Which brings us to your place, my place. We all have places of discontent and we're not hard pressed to name them. Whether they pertain to money, work, relationships, memories, frustrated dreams, most of us can answer right quickly what we wish we could change but cannot. Sometimes the sources of our discontent are due to circumstances that were always beyond our control; we were dealt a crummy hand. And sometimes the sources of our discontent are due to actual choices we have made— we chose the job, entered the relationship, took the path that led to this ordeal. It may change one day, but for now it will not. These are the cards we have been dealt, the cards perhaps that we dealt ourselves; and for now at least, we cannot exchange them. We are as locked in as the old apostle was. What do we do?

There is always the option of *Denial*. This is the fantasy option. We pretend. Instead of dealing with the disappointments we cover them with smiles or noise or with a flurry of frantic, constant busyness. If you were raised on Gospel Sunshine, this may be your problem. If you were spoonfed the notion that God's children shouldn't hurt and never break, then when something in you begins breaking, you paper it over with piety, you put on the plaster of Happy Hymns and Prayers, and you move on. Or if you are the more sensible, secular, tough-it-out type, you plaster on more work, more laughs, a few more drinks, and you move on. Either way, your life is an exhausting pretense that Everything Is Fine when it is not. And a great deal of your life goes unmet, unaddressed, unlived, as all available energy is devoted to maintaining the front.

This was the option first taken by the exiles of Israel when they found themselves in Babylon, where they did not wish to be. Comforters sprang up everywhere saying, "This is nothing, this is nothing. God will have us home tomorrow." Scripture calls these comforters false prophets. In contrast to their words, Jeremiah gave alternative counsel: "Thus says the Lord of hosts, 'Build houses where you are and plant gardens where you are. And seek the welfare of the city where I have sent you into exile, for in its welfare you will find your welfare.'" Real captivities can come to anyone, including the people of God. Some captivities are long.

Scripture's plain advice is to face the reality we are in, to tell the truth of our circumstance, to live in no fantasy but to live where we are. The option of denial is a dead end.

So there's another option for captives. It's the option of *Despair*, or as von Hügel had it, the option of sulking. Here the mind settles into bitterness or curdles into cynicism. Here we collapse in our captivity and will not get up. If the way of denial refuses to see the bad, the way of despair refuses to see anything else. Despair's voice can't stop saying, "If only things were different," can't get off the broken record of asking "Why me?" Here all hope is refused; we sink into pity for ourselves and contempt for all others. We hate the cards we have been dealt; if we cannot change them, then by God we won't play. We'll throw them or we will mutter or we'll keep a stony silence while we sit out the game. We may have to endure it but we'll never ever embrace it. This is the way of despair.

The problem with despair is that ultimately it is as dishonest as denial. It is dishonest about our hope, for if as we believe, there is a God, and if as we believe, God is good, there is more at work in our captivities than meets the eye. No matter how dark the place, no matter how hideous the circumstance, the hidden Hands of God are present, always at work to bring ultimate deliverance. There is no hard place that cannot be a holy place. Utter hopelessness is always premature. Despair is dishonest about our hope.

It is also dishonest about our freedom. We may have little freedom in choosing our circumstances; we have great freedom in choosing our spirit. We may have no choice about where we are; we have monumental choices about who we are. So you are locked into something unpleasant. Maybe somehow you asked for it and regret that you did. Maybe you did not ask for it at all, but there it is. Count all the ways you are not free. Mourn all the ways you are not free. But see in your hand: there is your final freedom and your greatest freedom, the freedom to choose what you make of this. My friend Grady Nutt used to say, "Maturity is playing the cards you've been dealt"—picking them up and making what choices you can for the best possible purpose.

This is the option of *Acceptance*. Sometimes we only get there on the far side of Denial and Despair. In fact you may have noticed that in speaking of denial, despair, and acceptance, I have been speaking of "stages" in the progression of grief. At first you cannot take in your loss; this is denial. Then you cannot take in anything else; this is despair. But the final stage of healthy grief is acceptance, where loss is acknowledged and life is acknowledged, where the door to what cannot be is closed and the door to what may now be done is opened. In such acceptance lies our greatest freedom and our only hope.

Listen to a true story.[3] Years ago near Christmastime a nursery school teacher told her students they could make Christmas presents for their parents. Each child could choose a gift to make for father or for mother. There was a boy in the class who loved his father very much. He knew his dad loved to smoke a pipe, and he wanted to make him an ashtray. The teacher helped him work the clay with his little hands till he got the clay in the right shape. It was hard work, but when it was done he was proud of how it looked. The teacher asked him what color he thought his dad might like. "Blue!" said the boy, and she gave him a brush and blue paint and he painted the ashtray bright blue. And when it was done he was proud of what he had made for his dad.

On the last day of school before Christmas the children put on a pageant and all the parents came. But the highlight of the day for the boy was not the pageant but the present. He could not wait for the moment to give his father what he had worked so hard to make for him. But when the moment came, somehow in the rush of running and waving and carrying a present and putting on a coat, the boy slipped and fell, and the ashtray shattered. For a moment he stared in terror and disbelief. Then his face melted and he crumpled to the floor and he cried and cried and cried.

His father was moved and tried to comfort him. He patted the boy's head and said, "Now that's all right. It really doesn't matter, son. It doesn't matter at all." But the boy's mother with a greater wisdom said, "Oh, but it does matter. It matters a great deal." And she sat on the floor with her son and held him in her

---

[3]I first heard this story told by John R. Claypool, who attributed it to William Muehl and gave details and application similar to what is here. Muehl relates a leaner version of the story in his book *Why Preach? Why Listen?* (Philadelphia: Fortress Press, 1986) 92.

arms, and she wept with him.

After a few minutes had passed and the sobbing had eased up and tears had been wiped away, the mother got a box and said to her son, "Now let's pick up all the pieces and take them home and see what we can make with what's left."

This is the gospel. Like the father's voice in the story there is a voice in the world and in us saying: "Don't cry, it doesn't matter." This is the voice of denial. Like the voice of the boy who cries inconsolably, there is another voice in the world and in us crying: "Nothing else matters at all." This is the voice of despair. But like the voice of the mother there is the voice of God, who bears with us the real losses of our lives, who weeps with us and waits with us and then goes on to say, "Now let's pick up the pieces and see what we can make of what's left." That is the voice of acceptance, both of loss and of life. And it is the gift of God, who in the beginning created from nothing, but who ever since has been creating out of broken pieces.

Has God not been bending and weeping over broken pieces since the beginning, and making wonders of what was left? Out of broken slaves were made the chosen people. Out of a broken King David was born the music of psalms. Out of a broken temple the prophets were lifted to new vision. Out of a broken covenant love shaped a New Covenant. And out of the broken body of Jesus Christ, out of God's own broken heart, was there not made at last a Resurrection and a Life? The Living God still bends and weeps and waits over all that is broken and cannot be mended—and even so is asking, "What can we make of the pieces?" To open the heart to such a God is to open the heart to the great gift of acceptance. Acceptance of losses and limits. Acceptance of life and a hope as huge as Easter.

—PDD

8

God's People
Are True Healers

Luke 10:25-37; Colossians 1:9-12

Comment

This sermon works from a unified concept of pain and of what it means to preach to pain. Note the refusal to render the Samaritan parable into either a "pastoral" or a "prophetic" text. Typically, preachers have opted for the latter, have thundered against compassionless religion and pled grayly for us all to go out and help "others." The alternative offered here, consistent with recent literary studies of this parable's "point of view," presents us with an embarrassment and a kinship: we are the helplessly wounded and the scandalously rescued and on that basis are liberated for lives of compassion. This compassion will be expressed both by initiatives toward other persons and by initiatives toward social and political structures. The sermon therefore seeks to do what the parable does with such genius: to gather all pain, and to place it all in the life of the listener. To keep such a sermon from death-by-abstraction, specific contemporary lives are adduced. What is more, some response is given to the question too seldom heard from the pulpit: "But how?" For this purpose, the preacher performs a new marriage of the Gospel text with the epistle text of the day.

The deadly bubonic plague struck the city of Oran. Because the disease was so contagious, Oran was quarantined: no one was allowed to leave and no one allowed to enter. The residents were left to do the best they could against the ravages of the disease. Some people suffered silently; others complained loudly. Some were heroic; others, manipulative. Some had compassion for the dying; others ignored them, while still others stole from them.

Oran's situation is fictional, for it is the setting for Camus's classic novel, *The Plague*. However, the human responses in that story are true to life. A conversation between two of the main characters helps to put those responses in perspective. Both men had done what they could to help the sick and dying, and late one evening, almost exhausted, they talked about the situation. The conversation moved to their understanding of life's purpose. One character concluded that life has diseases and victims; our goal, he said, is that we should at least not join forces with the diseases. Then he added a third category of human beings, those who are "the true healers." They are rare, and it is a difficult vocation, but true healers care for the victims and bring peace.[1]

There is a remarkable parallel between Camus' story and the parable of Jesus we heard this morning. It is perhaps Jesus' best known parable, and for that reason we have difficulty hearing it with any kind of freshness or imagining that anything new can be discovered in it. Let's give it a try. Let's begin by giving the parable a different name. It is well known as "The Parable of the Good Samaritan," but it might better be understood if we call it "The Parable of the Wounded Traveler."[2]

When we hear stories, most of us identify with one character or another, and then hear the story from that character's perspective. Most of us hear this parable from the perspective of the Samaritan, for we want very much to be like that Samaritan, caring for broken people around us. But let's hear it differently this morning.

You are a merchant on your way from Jerusalem to Jericho. The Jerusalem-Jericho road is a winding, narrow road; it is a dangerous road, for there are many places where robbers can hide to attack travelers. But you have a job to do, orders to take, merchandise to deliver, and so you proceed cautiously. You've done it before and not been robbed, but you've heard the horror stories of other traveling merchants. You've been lucky so far.

---

[1]Albert Camus, *The Plague*, trans. Stuart Gilbert (New York: Random House, 1948) 229-30.

[2]Suggested by Arthur C. McGill, *Suffering: A Test of Theological Method* (Philadelphia: Geneva, 1968) 103-106.

This time your luck runs out. Not only do they rob you, they severely beat you, and leave you for dead. Lying in the ditch semiconscious, you hope that someone will come along and help. Your luck has returned, for coming down the road is a priest. God must be with you, for this man will not only give you physical care but also offer you spiritual comfort during your recovery.

What! He looked this way, then moved onto the other side of the road and kept on walking! He saw you and ignored you. He didn't even speak a word of concern.

You moan as you begin to feel the heat of the day. In a little while you see another figure coming down the road. From his dress he appears to be a Levite, one of the assistants at the Temple. God's grace has shined on you for sure, for this fellow understands ordinary people. He's not so high and mighty in the religious hierarchy as to be out of touch with the needs of people in trouble. Sure enough, he is coming over to you. You are so weak that you cannot speak, and you try to look grateful as he bends over you. But he shakes his head, moves to the other side of the road, and walks away. Well, that's it! If those two religious types won't help you, there's no hope. With death holding you in its clutches, you lose consciousness.

A clomping sound awakens you. It is a donkey, carrying another traveler. You can't make out the fellow, but you expect no help. He stops and comes over to you. As he bends over you and touches your broken arm, you recognize that he is a Samaritan. You've had it now, for you are a Jew, and you're sure this Samaritan feels about you the same way you feel about him. You have got no use for Samaritans. They're blasphemous, morally suspect, and racially inferior. You've heard the stories of what Samaritans do to Jews they find alone. He's probably checking for any leftover valuables, and then he will smash in your head. Sure enough, he's going over to his donkey to get a club or a knife to finish you off. Now he's coming back. You wonder what he has in the bag.

Something is not right. He's pouring oil and wine on your wounds, and now he's bandaging them. You look into those Samaritan eyes, something you never thought you'd do, and you see compassion. You can't figure this guy out.

He picks you up carefully and slides you on the back of his donkey. Soon you arrive at a familiar inn. The Samaritan goes inside and soon returns with the innkeeper. Gently they lift you off the animal and take you to a room. They place you in the bed. The Samaritan stays with you for the night: feeding you, changing your bandages, and offering words of comfort.

When you awaken the next morning he and the innkeeper are standing beside your bed. He hands the innkeeper two silver coins and says, "Take care of him, and when I come back this way, I will pay you whatever else you spend on him." The Samaritan's compassionate eyes look into yours. He gently touches your shoulder and says "Shalom" (peace be with you), and leaves.

Each of us has been wounded, some of us more than others, but we all have been wounded. That is, at some point in our lives each of us has been overwhelmed, has fallen victim to something very painful: maybe physical disability, maybe emotional distress, maybe loss of a loved one, maybe disappointment in a relationship, maybe loss of a job or reputation, maybe lost opportunity, maybe being victimized by insult or humiliation—whatever it may have been, each of us has been wounded in some way.

And perhaps like this wounded traveler, those people whom you thought would help you only looked briefly at you and passed on the other side. And you wondered, "Do I have any true friends, any true neighbors—people who really care about me?"

The Good News of our faith is that there is someone who will bind up our wounds. That one, like the Samaritan, was despised by many people. He was religiously and morally suspect, but he does care for you. Yes, Christ is the Good Samaritan for all us wounded persons.

The result is that we are not only grateful patients but commissioned healers as well. Christ tells us at the end of the parable to "Go and do likewise," to be what Paul called "the Body of Christ"—Christ's representatives to the world. We, whose wounds have been bound by Christ the Good Samaritan, are sent out as Good Samaritans to bind the wounds of all peoples. Having been healed by the Christ, we are sent into the world to heal the diseased.

One of these Good Samaritans is a young woman who has struggled all of her life with low self-esteem. She has a great deal of difficulty believing that anyone could really like her. She assumes that she has no real talents. She doubts her value, despite the fact that she is a very bright, sensitive, and gifted person. Her pysche bears the scars of a family who could not affirm her appearance, her abilities, and her potential.

Yet by the grace of God that wounded young woman has the remarkable ability to help other persons deal with their low self-esteem. Because she understands their wounds, she is able to help them work through their problems with self-image. By God's grace this wounded person is also a Good Samaritan. She remains wounded in many ways, but despite those difficulties, she is at the same time able to bind the wounds of others. Though she remains diseased with a poor self-image, she has become a true healer. Perhaps she is able to be a true healer because she understands what it is like to be a victim of the disease.

This young woman is a fair analogy for the people of God, the Body of Christ. We are diseased with all kinds of afflictions: physical limitations, personality quirks, faulty moral perception, insensitivity, and other things which make us less than perfect healers. But by the grace of God we, God's people, can be true healers, even while we are wounded, just like this young woman. How do we avoid being crippled by the disease or simply remaining its victim? That is, how do we become true healers? To begin with, we must avoid taking the easy out, which is the role of spectator, a passerby like the priest or the Levite. We should be careful that we not view the priest or the Levite who walked by on the other side as villains. They were not evil; they were just spectators. They probably had 25 legitimate reasons not to help that wounded man. It would get them off their schedule of charitable activities planned for the day. The robbers might be hiding nearby to pounce on those giving aid. And so forth.

How do we avoid being spectators? Maybe Colossian's description of the worthy Christian life will be of some help. Chapter 1 gives three characteristics of that kind of life, a life which God can use for healing a wounded world. The characteristics sound rather ordinary: endurance, patience, and joy.

First, *endurance*. Endurance has to do with our response to events in our lives, courageously pressing on in spite of what comes our way. Sometimes we feel mortally wounded by people and circumstances. Christian endurance means working through that pain depending on God's strength. That does not mean that endurance will exclude anger, frustration, grief, or emotional disorientation. To the contrary, most likely, endurance *will include* some anger, frustration, grief, or emotional disorientation. But by God's ever-present grace, we can endure courageously, for God does sustain us, sometimes sustaining us through the Good Samaritan care of friends, family members, and psychologists.

Endurance can also have to do with less dramatic circumstances, but no less trying. For some people the very routine of their lives—long days of work, pressure for production, sleepless nights with a sick child, constant pain, a trying personal relationship, the boredom of retirement—this routine requires endurance. To endure means not to become absorbed in that routine. To endure means that we not lose our love for life under God.

We could learn much from those persons who care for our children during worship. Their endurance with our children—picking up toys, changing diapers, wiping runny noses, and changing sheets—that endurance is a testimony to the love which ought to be part of our routine, whatever it is. Those who endure can be true healers.

Second, the characteristic of *patience*. Patience has to do with our relationships with other persons. People are wonderful, but people can also be the biggest pain! At the end of each semester many professors confide in their colleagues that "teaching could be wonderful, if it just weren't for the students!" It is delightful to relate to people like us, to friendly people, to tolerant people. It is not so easy to relate to insecure people, to manipulative people, or to people we consider boring, unlovely, or irresponsible. Only by God's grace can we exercise patience with these trying relationships and bring healing to their lives.

Patience means putting away our judgmental arrogance and practicing a humility which tries to understand from the other person's viewpoint. Often we cannot know the private hells in which other persons live. Two real persons' lives illustrate the problem.

By all appearances to her colleagues at work, she is self-indulging, opinionated, quick-tempered, and overbearing. Yet for those few persons who have the patience to get to know her, she is a hardworking person who wants to help people. Only a handful of people have any inkling of her inner turmoil: her lonely struggle to find friends as she worries that they will think the worst of her; her grief shared with her husband that they could never have children; her fear of retirement's isolation.

Or consider the middle-aged man whom most people regard as obnoxious. He tries too hard to be funny; he speaks his mind and often offends his friends, though unintentionally. He relates very awkwardly to most women as he tries to impress them. He is one of those persons you can enjoy but only in small doses. Very few people know about his childhood of physical abuse or his insecurities about his physical appearance.

Compassion growing out of patience, recognizing that we are wounded also, will allow us to relate to people like this. You know people like them in our community, perhaps even within this community of faith. Patience is not gritting our teeth; it is opening up the possibilities for relationship. Patience means learning to live with other persons' imperfections; patience must be more than tolerance; patience is acting in grace. With patience we can be true healers.

Finally, the characteristic of *joy*. There is nothing shallow about joy. Christian joy includes laughter, joke telling, and fun; but Christian joy is not an emptyheaded grin, a frozen smile in the face of life's challenges. Rather it is the joy which has embraced life under God despite the wounds. Witness the joy in Jesus' life, who despite accusations and rejection by his hometown neighbors, was able to celebrate at banquets and hug little children. He and his disciples were not grim, but full of life, full of joy. Only a person living with this kind of joy could so freely risk and determinedly love as the Good Samaritan.

This joy grows out of a passion for life under God. Spectators do not know this kind of joy, for they seek only stability. With stability as their primary objective, the passion for life is absent, and so is true joy. Passion distinguishes joy from pleasantness. Spectators can be pleasant, for that is stabilizing. In contrast to pleasantness, joy is passionate and willing to take risks. With joy we can be true healers.

Most of our emphasis this morning has concerned the need for healing in personal relationships, but we would be sticking our heads in the sand and ignoring the gospel if we did not recognize the wounds resulting from social and political relationships. As much as we might like to, we cannot be spectators in a world so overrun with violence and injustice. People are literally bleeding in this world, and God's people must help to bind up their wounds.

It is difficult for God's people to speak with one voice on these issues, for we are diverse in our politics and social commitments. Nevertheless, we must try in whatever way we can to bind up these wounds caused by violence and injustice. We must try to be instrumental in healing the diseases brought on by social injustice, political strife, and the nuclear threat. While we may not be able to speak with one voice, we must discuss these issues with each other; and then with all our differences come together to heal the wounds which plague the modern world. If we cannot speak or do something to bring healing, we have become like the priest and Levite who passed by the wounded man because they were too busy taking care of internal business. We and our world are diseased; we are wounded. Endurance, patience, and joy will not remove all the disease or heal all the wounds. But like the Good Samaritan, endurance, patience and joy will allow us to become true healers where we are on the road.

Rise up, God's people! Saddle your donkeys and keep your eyes open, for life's ditches are strewn with wounded people. With endurance, patience, and joy, you—God's people—can be true healers.

— DND

9

Three Faces at Easter

John 20:1-18

Comment

Preaching on Easter Sunday presents unusual challenges and opportunities for "Gathering" the listeners. The congregation is larger and more diverse than usual. Many are unaccustomed to the working partnership of hearing sermons. Distractions abound. To be heard by this annual gangly crowd, the sermon must be, in some ways, remedial. To touch them where the Resurrection means to touch them, the sermon must address real death, alienation, pain. To be faithful to the News of this day, the sermon must sing. The text for this sermon provides a happy opportunity for a simple structure and a broad inclusion of needs and responses to the Easter tidings.

We include this sermon not only because it addresses unresolved confusion (Peter) and grief (Mary Magdalene), but because it also addresses the gift of faith apart from pain (the beloved disciple). Preachers sensitized to the issues of pain may forget that not everyone in the room is in the grip of a struggle. The gospel is big enough to include happy children and fortunate saints whose faith is cheerful and serene. This is added hope for the wounded: the gospel's agenda is vaster than our pain.

I have news. The Lord is risen. He is risen indeed.

You knew I was going to say that. We all came here knowing we'd hear it. We've all come to the same place at the same time, knowing we would hear the same word. I suppose we all wanted in some way to hear it, or we would not have come.

But it stands to reason that this announcement—the Lord is risen—strikes all of us differently. Each of us brought with us to church today a different past, a different mood, a different need, a different life. Some of you are happy and hopeful. Some of you are sad. Some have finished with something: for you the night is over, you have emerged. Some are still in the middle of something, feeling your way through the dark. Some of you have found somebody wonderful to walk with. Some of you are lonely, walking by yourself. Some of you are practically glowing with big faith. Some of you are down to a little scrap of faith, holding on for dear life. Some of you have not yet found a faith, but something in you wishes you could. Some of you once had more faith but the lights went out and you're groping to find it again. We come here with many different histories and shapes of faith.

Will you notice this about the Gospel accounts of the first Easter? The sun came up that day on men and women whose hearts were in different places. Each of them who heard the news had a different life, gave a different answer. Each Easter appearance is different because the risen Christ finds His children in such different places. He surprises the socks off every one. But each encounter is unique, each response has a different shape— for that's the way we are.

The Gospel of John shows us three faces of Easter morning. Three people stand at the same empty tomb. Each of them finds a faith, but each by a different path, each in a different form. Study these three faces. One of them may bear some resemblance to your own face, may give a clue to finding your own shape of Easter faith.

Now the story starts in a cemetery in the dark. There is a woman there, Mary Magdalene. She has come to visit the grave of Jesus. To her astonishment and dismay the grave is open and empty. We can't see her face, not yet; it's too dark. And she runs away, she runs to two friends to give them this raw data: the stone has been moved, the corpse is gone, no one knows where it is.

Whereupon these two friends—Simon Peter and the one referred to as the disciple Jesus loved—these two start running to the cemetery. Ever notice how much running there is in the Easter stories? Mary runs, Peter runs, the beloved disciple runs. Maybe on Easter we should run to church—or drive real fast! Maybe when the choir and the ministers process at Easter we should all sprint down the aisle, hair flying, robes flapping. Don't forget where this running occurs—a cemetery. I go to cemeteries quite often. Nobody ever runs there. In a cemetery we always walk, slowly. We're always hushed, we always tread carefully through the monuments of memory; we walk softly, on our hearts. Can you think of a more striking sign that today's news really changes everything? Running in the cemetery!

Now one of them—and only one of them—is apparently running for joy. One of them puts it all together very quickly and flies to his faith: the beloved disciple. He and Peter have a footrace to the tomb and he wins hands down. He looks in, sees the grave clothes lying there; and as soon as Peter arrives and they both go inside, he believes. He sees a little evidence, no proof, just a small sign or two; and his heart tells him—Christ is risen. Ask him: How do you know? He'll say: I don't know, but I do.

Don't call him naive. Call him fortunate. The Gospel calls him Beloved. For a long time he'd had a special kind of relationship with Jesus. Everywhere you look in John's Gospel, he is close to him, leaning on him. When I imagine the face of this disciple looking into the tomb, I see a bright face, a fortunate face, a face with not many scars on it if you know what I mean. Some lives are like that.

Not long ago I mentioned in a sermon that a great many people, including many in this congregation, have been abused. When I said so, it got very quiet in the room. After the service a friend coming out my door said, "Should I feel guilty that I've never been abused, that my life has been wonderful?" The answer is, Heavens no! Sometimes in a church like this we speak so much to the struggles of life that people who are not struggling must begin to wonder if something is wrong with them! Heavens no. Life is not always a struggle. For some people faith is not a struggle. The New Testament indicates that some people have a special gift for faith—they're "wired" for it. And, let's face it, many of us arrive at certain miraculous moments when faith does come easy—easier than usual. Who can explain it? Sometimes an unexpected door to the heart swings open—we simply know. If such a moment comes to you, lean into it. If a door to new faith swings open for you, walk through the door. Sometimes, as Pascal said, "the heart has reasons that reason cannot know." Honor your heart's reasons. This is how the beloved dsciple experienced Easter. He saw an empty tomb, that was all, and he knew.

But his friend Peter was with him—and he did not know. He was in the same place, entered the same tomb, saw the same evidence—then scratched his head and went home. He didn't get it. It would come together for him later, but on Easter morning it did not. Why not? I don't know. He was a different person. Maybe it was his temperament. Maybe it was his experience.

His most recent experience was massive guilt. He had broken his promise to Jesus, abandoned him. His final act toward his friend was to scream that he never knew him. He had been weeping ever since. Now Sunday morning comes and he's running, but he's running on guilty feet. The other disciple outruns him—you do not run so well when you're guilty. Remember the song that said "I'm never gonna' dance again / Guilty feet ain't got no rhythm"? Guilty feet are not too swift either. Feelings of guilt, like many other feelings, can make us slow to respond in faith. He's feeling very small. When you're feeling tiny it takes time to believe that God's love is huge. It takes a little time for some. It's all right.

Maybe you're in a similar circumstance. You've come to check out this news of an empty tomb. And here in church you see some people glowing and singing like beloved disciples. You're not glowing, not yet. There are unfinished feelings—guilt perhaps; or some other wound is in your way. It's all right. See what you can see. Confess what you know to confess. Open your heart to what you can. In time if you are honest and receptive, if something in you is willing to keep searching and keep waiting, it will come. Has God not said, "If with all your heart you seek me you will surely find me"? John says it was seven days till the risen Christ appeared to Peter and opened him up with a painful question and freed him of his guilt and gave him a calling so big he couldn't feel small anymore. Christ can open a tomb more quickly than he can open the bruised hearts of some. One face of Easter is to see what you can, confess what you can, and wait.

But look at one more face. Not a face of serene belief like the beloved disciple. Not a face of waiting like Peter. Here's a face streaming with tears of grief. Mary Magdalene comes back to the tomb and she cries and she cries. It's not guilt that's in her way. If she'd had any issue of guilt in her life Jesus had dealt with it long ago. She's just sad. Someone she loves has been taken away and she doesn't understand.

A stranger is there and asks her, "Woman, why are you weeping?" The stranger is grinning from ear to ear, an angel. But Mary can't see that; she has tears in her eyes. She turns away. There is another stranger who asks her, more tenderly, "Woman why are you weeping?" You know who it is? *You* know who it is. I know who it is. It's the One she was crying for. It's the One who has come to wipe every tear from her eyes, to put all joy in her heart, all music in her voice. The one Face in the world she'd give anything to see is leaning over her. But there are tears in her eyes. She can't see.

The beloved disciple needed only a little evidence. Peter needed more—a personal encounter. But for Mary even the presence of Christ does not break through. We can be so grief-stricken, so despondent, that even Christ's own presence beside us is not enough to clear the fog and lift the terrible weight. What does it take? He knew. "Mary."

She needed to hear him call her name. What does it mean to hear the living Christ call your name? It's a way of hearing him say: I know you as no one else knows you; I know where you've been and where you are, the meaning of every tear, the secret of every sadness; and I am with you, I love you, I am calling you. That is what Mary heard when she heard her name on Sunday morning. And it cleared her vision and it sent her running with the news—"I have seen the Lord!"

It is not in my power to give anyone here the experience of hearing Christ call your name. But I will tell you what I believe. I believe He is here. I believe He is alive and is more real in this room than I am. Some of you know this, because like the beloved disciple you have been given the gift of knowing it. Some of you, like Peter, do not know it yet but you will know it soon if you watch for Him and wait for Him. But are not there also some to whom He comes today with a new presence of tenderness and power to wipe away your tears by the calling of your name? No one will hear Him call your name but you. I can only ask in his name that you listen for your name. Listen. . . . Those who with all their hearts will listen for the Voice, in time will hear their name, will find their reason to say and to sing—"I have seen the Lord."

Happy Easter.

—*PDD*

10

Cultivating Passionate Faith

Mark 1:35-45; 11:15-17

Comment

As was affirmed in chapter 2, the faith community's response to pain will be deeply rooted in their vision of God's response to pain. Here is a sermon designed to focus that vision, and to focus in particular upon the eyes of God, fiery with passion. For Christians the word passion *rightly has as its central association the suffering of Jesus in the hours surrounding his crucifixion. The sorrows of his death, however, are not the only image we have of his essential passion. Here is a sermon which proclaims that passion from a strong text of a different kind, one that precludes all possibility of sentimentalism.*

The sermon's aim is, by lifting up the pathos of God, to strengthen the pathos of the faith community, to stir them to an answering passion and compassion. The language used in the service of such a theme can and should take some risks, as is done here. Still, one risk will not be taken; the danger of confusing pathos with undisciplined feeling is great enough in our culture to warrant a strong counterpoint, with the help of a beagle, on the difference between focused passion and mere enthusiasm.

Your gaze is drawn to the top left corner of the painting. The man's left fist is tightly clenched; his neck is stiff; and his torso is coiled for delivering another blow with the whip of cords gripped in his strong right hand. His brow is furrowed; his jaw is set; and his mouth is angrily downturned.

But it is mostly his eyes which captivate you. They seem to cut into the souls of the people who are fleeing his anger. Piercing eyes. Eyes full of anger and pain and intensity of purpose. These eyes are passionate eyes, eyes which reflect the depths of the man's soul.

They are the eyes of Jesus, Jesus in the moment of exploding anger against the injustice of the moneychangers and merchants. The eyes of Jesus in a moment only rarely portrayed by artists, but once again the master Rembrandt has frozen that powerful moment on his canvas, visualizing the depth of Jesus' emotions. These are not the familiar eyes of Jesus—you know, those soft and harmless eyes of the popular Jesus paintings, the eyes and person of one who seeks otherworldly bliss.

Rembrandt captures the passion of that moment, and it is true to who Jesus was and the sort of people Jesus calls us to be. It is no wonder we haven't known what to do with Jesus' aggressive action in the Temple. His action seems out of character with those traditional sentimental portraits of the gentle, passive teacher, telling parables on the hillsides of first century Galilee. Yet most of us also privately relish this story of this Jesus who kicks some tail to get people to listen to him. Let us be clear as the text is clear. Jesus does not make a scene in the Temple to call attention to himself. He is not engaged in vengeful retaliation or aggressive domination. He is acting passionately in behalf of others. By driving out the merchants and forbidding people to use the Temple as a thoroughfare, he is reclaiming for the Gentiles their place of worship in the Temple. The Gospel writer makes this abundantly clear in Jesus' ringing denunciation: "My house shall be a house of prayer *for all nations* but you have made it a den of thieves." Jesus is not rejecting the forms of worship in the Temple nor the useful services which these merchants offered. He is objecting passionately to their insensitivity to the spiritual needs of Gentiles, who have lost their only place of worship due to the needs of the marketplace. Supply and demand had run roughshod over spiritual well-being.

O.K., even if we understand his reasons, why did Jesus choose to behave in such a rowdy manner? Why make such a scene and unnecessarily offend people who might have been sympathetic to appeals for gradual reform of the Temple? Where is reason in all this? Where is the tranquility which religion is supposed to offer? Did he wake up that morning and decide that he had reached his limit? Was this something done in a spontaneous moment of rage?

Did he just need some merchants "to make his day"?

Actually if we consider all the descriptions of Jesus' life, we discover a person who passionately loved God and any person he encountered. The Gospel writer Mark emphasizes Jesus' visceral responses to people in need. For example, Jesus acted out of the same kind of passion in healing the leper. We would do well to listen again to Mark's very brief description of that encounter.

Jesus gets up before dawn to be alone with his God. Simon and the others seek him out and remind him that he is famous locally and many people want an audience. Jesus' response is "Let's go elsewhere, to the neighboring villages, so I can preach there too, because that is why I came." Then the narrator tells us that Jesus proceeded to preach *and* cast out demons. The urgency of his message was always accompanied by urgent action. Then along comes a leper, on his knees "pleading," "begging" Jesus to heal him. Now hear the sequence of Jesus' response to the leper's plea for help. First, Jesus is "filled or moved with pity," or as the word literally means: he was torn up in his guts by this individual's cry for help.

It is interesting that one of the ancient manuscripts of that text states that "Jesus was angry" rather than "Jesus was moved to pity." Indeed, Jesus was angry at the dehumanizing way leprosy had thwarted God's good creation in this man. Whatever the text, it is the same basic reaction by Jesus to the man's affliction; Jesus is viscerally stirred up by the man's disfiguring disease.

And so, says Mark, Jesus then "stretches out his hand." Jesus takes the initiative for contract with an untouchable, a leper, the first century's equivalent of an AIDS victim. Indeed Jesus does touch the leper. Next, Jesus responds to the leper's earlier statement of belief, that Jesus could cure him if he wanted to. Jesus says, "Of course, I want to cure you" (Phillips translation). Finally, Jesus says, "Be clean." Gut-wrenching passion, holding out the hand, touching, expressing the desire to help, and finally doing something to alleviate the hurt—that is the sequence. This is not a complicated decision-making process. Jesus' action comes from a heart of *habitual* passion which stirs his insides before speech and action are evident.

So how can we cultivate that kind of passionate faith? Where does such passion come from? Jesus said "follow me," and he shows us the way.

Again, look into the eyes of Jesus and you can see God. Look into the eyes of Jesus and you see the people of the world. Look into the eyes of Jesus and you see passionate love for God. Look into the eyes of Jesus and you can see passionate love for people.

Those eyes are not the glazed over eyes of those who relish their private love affair with God. They are not the eyes of the self-righteous, self-appointed religious generals who wage holy battle to identify the sheep and goats. They are not the eyes of the passive individual who thinks religion is a nice idea. They are the eyes of passion. They are eyes with outreaching arms, an open heart, with feet ready for action. They are the eyes of love, not sentimental, not judgmental, not self-serving, not private versions of "love." They are the eyes of God's love. They are eyes of sparking anger when "the least of these" are mistreated. They are tear-filled eyes for God's little ones who grieve. They are laughing eyes celebrating small accomplishments. They are understanding eyes for those confused. They are eyes of hope for those despairing. They are *com*passionate eyes fixed in sockets of holy passion.

That's what it all comes down to. A passionate faith yields compassionate persons. Passionate love for God yields compassion for people, true compassion which responds to others, willing to risk misunderstanding, willing to appear inconsistent, willing to be labeled "odd" or "peculiar."

No doubt, the leper saw this quality in Jesus' eyes. We do, too. There is something else about those eyes. They are the eyes of one who has shared pain. Jesus' dramatic action in the Temple did not issue from an ego which was fed up and then exploded. Jesus did not overturn the moneychangers' tables and drive out the merchants in order to vent personal frustration at social incompetencies. His was not the anger of frustration which blows off steam and says, "Whew! I feel better now." His radical action grew out of his passionate identification with outcasts in his culture. The insult and indifference to the Gentiles' place of worship prodded him to action. His is an anger growing out of passion and compassion for the victimized people. It is anger issuing from the love of God.

Thus we come to the significance of Jesus' action for our lives. His was a focused passion. It was passion directed to loving God and as a result passion directed to caring for people.

The difficulty is that we often mistake enthusiasm for passion. A simple illustration will clarify the difference. We have a new puppy at our house—a little eight-week-old beagle named Wendy. She is full of life: gnawing at the furniture, nipping at our heels, running here and there, wetting randomly, and yelping when she doesn't get attention. One might say Wendy has a real passion for life. Actually it's not passion; it's just an unfocused enthusiasm. Her enthusiasm isn't a bad thing, though listening to her three a.m. howls is a bit irritating. The point is that for all the energy she expends and all the enthusiasm she displays for life around her, she's not really passionate for any real purpose. And it's not just because she is a dog. Human creatures often mistake their enthusiasm and energy for passion. They hurry here and there; they are concerned about problems and issues, but they aren't focused on people. They may be very enthusiastic about correct religious doctrine, or authentic religious experiences, or the well-being of religious institutions, or even solving the moral problems of the world. Yet their lives are not passionately focused on their God or God's children. Passion has to do with persons. Their enthusiasm and energy are impersonal.

You see, it is not the religious professionals and heroes who are necessarily the passionate lovers of God and God's creatures. There were plenty of religious folk in Jesus' day, sincere to their toes about maintaining true religion, but for all their energy and enthusiasm, they were indifferent to lepers and foreigners who needed to worship in the Temple. In theory and in their hearts they believed that they cared about those folk, but because they lacked focused passion, they could not be compassionate.

Let me make a direct appeal to you—to us. In this community we value harmony, tolerance, and understanding—all worthy values as far as they go. Often, too often, in the pursuit of these worthy values we are satisfied with being simply pleasant, predictable, and prudent, none of which encourages passion. What would happen if we came out of our safe closets to work at living as a truly passionate community? Could we stand a community
 of mystics and seekers?
  activists and charismatics?
  radicals and comedians?

dreamers and dancers?

The passionate eyes of Christ may yet draw us out into the open of God's marvelous creation. Imagine what we would be if we passionately loved God with our minds, hearts, souls and strength? As Jesus said, we will love our neighbor as ourselves.

—DND